Gerd Kaiser

Stundenblätter Hemingway Short Stories

Indian Camp / The Killers / The Battler / Old Man at the Bridge

41 Seiten Beilage

Ernst Klett Verlag

Reihe Stundenblätter Englisch

Die in den Stundenblättern besprochenen Kurzgeschichten finden sich in folgenden Lektüreheften bzw. Oberstufenlesebüchern.

CIP-Kurztitelaufnahme der Deutschen Bibliothek

Kaiser, Gerd:
Stundenblätter Hemingway short stories:
Indian camp, The killers, The battler, Old man at the bridge / Gerd Kaiser. –
2. Aufl. – Stuttgart: Klett, 1986. & Beil.
  (Reihe: Stundenblätter Englisch)
  ISBN 3-12-925151-0

ISBN 3-12-925151-0

2. Auflage 1986
Alle Rechte vorbehalten
Fotomechanische Wiedergabe nur mit Genehmigung des Verlages
© Ernst Klett Verlage GmbH u. Co. KG, Stuttgart 1984
Satz: G. Müller, Heilbronn; Wilhelm Röck, Weinsberg
Druck: Wilhelm Röck, Weinsberg
Einbandgestaltung: Zembsch' Werkstatt, München

Inhalt

Fachwissenschaftliche und fachdidaktische Aspekte

Hemingways Short Stories im Englischunterricht der Klassen 10 und 11

Kurzgeschichten haben spätestens ab Klasse 9 ihren festen Platz im Englischunterricht und erfreuen sich allgemein großer Beliebtheit. Die Schüler mögen Short Stories wegen ihrer Kürze und der damit verbundenen inhaltlichen Überschaubarkeit; für den Lehrer ist die Lektüre verschiedener Kurzgeschichten organisatorisch und methodisch einfacher zu bewältigen als etwa das extensive Lesen eines Romans oder mehrerer längerer Erzählungen. Zudem läßt sich mit der Behandlung von Kurzgeschichten auf der Mittelstufe eine Art Propädeutik der Textarbeit leisten, die dann der Arbeit mit literarischen Texten in den folgenden Jahren zugute kommt. So verfügen die Schüler in der 10. Klasse bereits über ein bescheidenes Interpretationsvokabular, das in der Folge ständig erweitert wird.

Unter dem vielfältigen Angebot amerikanischer und angelsächsischer Short Stories nehmen die Kurzgeschichten Hemingways seit langem eine Spitzenstellung ein, weil sie sich in besonderem Maße inhaltlich und sprachlich für die Behandlung im Englischunterricht eignen.

Die für dieses Heft ausgewählten Kurzgeschichten stellen in ihrer Abfolge eine sinnvolle Unterrichtseinheit dar. Drei Nick-Adams-Stories, in denen jeweils ein prägnantes Initiationserlebnis gestaltet wird und die inhaltlich aufeinander folgen, werden kontrastiv durch eine Short Story ergänzt, in der es nicht um die Realitätserfahrung eines heranwachsenden Jugendlichen, sondern um das Schicksal eines alten Mannes im Krieg geht.

Das Hauptinteresse liegt bei Nick Adams, einer Gestalt Hemingways, die in vielen Geschichten in verschiedenen Stationen seines Lebens wiederkehrt, und die im Erleiden mannigfaltiger psychischer und physischer Verwundungen von manchen Kritikern als der typisch Hemingwaysche „Held" angesehen wird. In der Kurzgeschichte „Indian Camp" (1925) ist Nick noch ein Kind, das unvermittelt Zeuge einer auf doppelte Weise blutigen Szene wird, indem er fast gleichzeitig eine primitive Kaiserschnittoperation in einem Indianerlager und den Selbstmord des jungen Indianervaters miterleben muß und so mit einer Wirklichkeit konfrontiert wird, die er noch nicht zu verarbeiten vermag. – In der Short Story „The Killers" (1927) ist Nick bereits älter; als Jugendlicher ist er in einem einfachen kleinstädtischen Straßenlokal zugegen, als bezahlte Killer kaltblütig den Mord eines erwarteten Gastes vorbereiten. Das Geschehen dieser knapp zwei Stunden, verbunden mit der Erkenntnis seiner Unfähigkeit zu helfen und zu retten, bringt Nick schließlich zu dem Entschluß, die Stadt zu verlassen. – In der Geschichte „The Battler" (1927) befindet sich Nick als Tramp unterwegs und muß erneut die Erfahrung machen, daß menschliche Existenz nicht ohne Mißtrauen, Brutalität und Kampf möglich ist, obschon Nick auch in der merkwürdigen Begegnung mit dem verrückten ehemaligen Preisboxer und seinem glatten Negerbegleiter manche paradoxe Widersprüchlichkeit noch nicht begreifen kann. – In eine völlig andere Welt führt Hemingways „Old Man at the Bridge" (1938), mit 760 Wörtern eine seiner kürzesten Short Stories. Die letztlich sinnlose Flucht eines alten Mannes im spanischen Bürgerkrieg vor der heranrückenden Artillerie variiert noch einmal die Grundfrage Hemingways nach der Möglichkeit, menschlich in einer unmenschlichen Welt zu leben.

In ihrer Gesamtheit vermitteln diese vier Kurzgeschichten einen Eindruck von der Kunst Hemingways.

Eine nicht unwesentliche Rolle bei der Auswahl der Geschichten spielte ihre leichte Verfügbarkeit. Alle hier besprochenen Texte sind in Schülerausgaben zugänglich.

„Indian Camp" ist abgedruckt in „Stories of Initiation", Klett Lektüren Nr. 5784; „The Killers" findet sich in „The Killers and Other Short Stories", Schöningh Graded Readers Nr. 43116; „The Battler" in der Schöningh Ausgabe, ferner in „Five Modern American Short Stories", Diesterwegs Neusprachliche Bibliothek, Nr. 482.

„Old Man at the Bridge" ist abgedruckt in „Modern Life", Revised Edition, Klett Nr. 5089 und in der Schöningh-Ausgabe.

Wenn alle vier Geschichten nacheinander als eine Unterrichtseinheit „Hemingway" behandelt werden sollen, empfiehlt es sich, die Besprechung der Geschichten nicht in der vorgeschlagenen Ausführlichkeit vorzunehmen, damit die gesamte Einheit nicht zu viel Zeit beansprucht.

Es ist aber keineswegs beabsichtigt zu empfehlen, die vier Hemingway-Kurzgeschichten unbedingt hintereinander im Unterricht zu behandeln. Vielmehr sind die in den Stundenblättern ausgearbeiteten Unterrichtsentwürfe zu den Short Stories als Bausteine gedacht, die je nach Einsatzmöglichkeit verwendet werden können. Das Bausteinprinzip ermöglicht es beispielsweise, in einer themaorientierten Unterrichtseinheit unterschiedliche Kurzgeschichten verschiedener Autoren zu lesen und zueinander in Beziehung setzen zu lassen. Drei Beispiele von Textsequenzen:

a) Unterrichtseinheit „Stories of Initiation" (etwa: Jessamyn West, Live Life Deeply; Hemingway, The Killers; John Steinbeck, Flight);

b) Unterrichtseinheit zur Kontaktarmut und Vereinsamung alter Menschen (etwa: Pinter, Request Stop; Pinter, Last to Go; Hemingway, A Clean, Well-Lighted Place; Hemingway, Old Man at the Bridge);

c) Unterrichtseinheit zur Eltern-Kind-Problematik (etwa: Hemingway, A Day's Wait; Frank O'Connor, My Oedipus Complex; Salinger, Down at the Dinghy; Hemingway, Indian Camp).

Die hier vorgestellten Kurzgeschichten eignen sich nach Thematik und inhaltlichem Schwierigkeitsgrad für die Klassen 10 und 11.

Zum Abschluß einer Unterrichtseinheit „Hemingway Short Stories" könnten den Schülern die zusammenfassenden Bemerkungen R. Gigers und J. Bensons (vgl. S. 9) zur Stellungnahme vorgelegt werden. Auch eignen sich die beiden Texte des Arbeitsblatts als Grundlage für eine Übersetzungsübung. (In diesem Zusammenhang sei angemerkt, daß es Schülern Spaß macht, dialogische Passagen aus Hemingways Kurzgeschichten gelegentlich ins Deutsche zu übersetzen und dabei den stark umgangssprachlichen Lapidarstil Hemingways möglichst treffend im deutschen Jargon wiederzugeben.)

Falls die Schüler über Leben und Werk Hemingways in großen Zügen informiert werden sollen, der Lehrer diese Aufgabe aber nicht einem Schüler-Referat überlassen möchte, so kann der Text auf S. 10/11 vervielfältigt vorgelegt und gelesen werden.

Hemingway's best writing attests to the fact that he has exploited the full range of devices at his disposal to open our minds and hearts as widely as possible; he has made us his fellow-workers and accomplices in the eternal quest for truth. If we are prepared to search patiently for signs and hints (sometimes presented with a finesse that renders them almost imperceptible), we will be brought into the presence of a literature unlike any other. By steeping ourselves in it and acquainting ourselves with its richness of verbal association and symbolism, we will soon find that he is giving us something far more definite than we expected to get at any first reading... But the full value and enjoyment of what we read can only be obtained if we make the most of our powers of projection. For, and that is the true secret of his art, he never makes the pattern of human existence that underlies his work clearly visible; he gives us only the rough outlines of it so that we are enticed into elaborating and completing it ourselves.

Romeo Giger, The Creative Void, Francke Verlag Bern, 1977, p. 102.

Commencing with "Indian Camp" and "Big Two-Hearted River" in 1924, Hemingway's prose takes a new direction in which repetition plays an important part. The foundation is newspaper prose – short sentences, direct statement, and simplified diction. But working from this foundation, the prose has been hardened and sharpened: it is both more intense and more formal, as well as more abstract. The formality is not that of literary prose, but that of oral literature. The emphasis is on simple words with a history, words that are haunted with associations which date back to man's earliest experiences with nature. Every Hemingway story, even the story with comic elements, is tragic. The tragedy of a modern event is given a timeless, mythic quality as the flat, impersonal, simplified prose, punctuated and structured by repetition, recounts the inevitable doom that overtakes nearly anonymous people in nearly anonymous settings.

Jackson J. Benson, E. Hemingway as a Short Story Writer, in: Hemingway, Wissenschaftliche Buchgesellschaft Darmstadt 1980, p. 362.

Allgemeines zum methodischen Vorgehen

Wenn fremdsprachliche Literatur im Unterricht behandelt wird, kann nicht eine alle Details berücksichtigende akademische Interpretation Ziel des Vorgehens sein. Vielmehr werden wir uns mit einer den Fähigkeiten der Schüler angepaßten „schulischen Interpretation" (Mihm) begnügen. Die schulische Interpretation setzt sich als Aufgabe, die Schüler im entdeckenden Lesen zu üben und sie zu möglichst reger Eigentätigkeit im Literaturunterricht zu führen. Die im Unterrichtsgespräch aufgeworfenen Fragestellungen sollen die Schüler dazu bringen, im Laufe der Zeit immer genauer zu lesen, relevante Einzelheiten zu berücksichtigen, stilistische Eigenheiten zu sehen, Bedeutungen zu erspüren, Mehrdeutigkeiten zu erkennen, ein Problembewußtsein zu entwickeln.

Schulische Interpretation heißt keineswegs, daß überwiegend die Schüler das Niveau der Texterarbeitung bestimmen und der Unterricht unter Umständen auf die reine Wiedergabe des Inhaltlichen hinausläuft. Voraussetzung für erfolgversprechende Textarbeit ist, daß die sogenannte „akademische" Interpretation zunächst einmal vom Lehrer bei seiner Unterrichtsvorbereitung geleistet wird. Anhand dessen, was dem Lehrer bei seiner Erstlektüre des Textes aufgefallen ist, was er dann beim wiederholten Lesen bemerkt, unterstrichen, notiert hat, und was schließlich durch hinzugezogene Sekundärliteratur ergänzt wird, ergibt sich sein eigenes Textverständnis. Dieses stellt dann die Basis sowohl für seine Lernzielbestimmungen als auch für seine methodische Planung im einzelnen dar. Er wird entscheiden, ob die Schüler größeren Gewinn durch extensives Lesen des Textes haben oder durch intensive Lektüre, ob der ganze Text auf einmal gelesen werden soll, oder schrittweise in genau zu bestimmenden Abschnitten. Er wird eine Zeitplanung vornehmen, die Unterrichtsinhalte und Unterrichtsformen der einzelnen Stunden entsprechend vorsehen, eventuell Zusatzmaterial bereitstellen. Er wird sich Leitfragen überlegen und Fragestellungen zu wichtigen Textstellen notieren. Immer wieder wird er nach der Möglichkeit von Brückenschlägen zur Erfahrungswelt der Schüler suchen, wird sich überlegen, wo Schüler aus persönlicher Betroffenheit ihre eigenen Fragestellungen miteinbringen könnten. Überhaupt wird er sich darum bemühen, das Unterrichtsgespräch so zu gestalten, daß die Schüler ständig ihre eigenen

Ernest Hemingway: Some Biographical Facts

Ernest Hemingway was born as the second of six children in Oak Park, a suburb of Chicago, Illinois, on July 21, 1899. His father, a medical doctor, used to take him out hunting and fishing and thus fostered his love for outdoor living.

After attending Oak Park High School for some years Ernest Hemingway left Chicago in 1917 and went to Kansas City where he became a reporter on the local newspaper, the "Star". Here he was trained to write brisk, short, informative prose.

Soon afterwards he voluntarily flung himself into the middle of the European war theatre of World War I, where he was active as a Red Cross driver in Austria and Italy. In 1918 Hemingway was badly wounded in Italy – an event that deeply influenced his later life and work.

After the war Hemingway went back to the USA, but soon returned to Europe as correspondent of the "Toronto Star". He started writing poetry and short stories in the early Twenties, and in 1925 published a collection of short stories under the title "In Our Time". It was not until 1926 though that Hemingway became generally known when his first novel "The Sun Also Rises" became a great success. It was understood as a mirror of the "lost generation"; the experience of the senselessness of war, and ultimately of life, lent pessimistic undertones to the book. Another collection of short stories, "Men Without Women" came out in 1927, most of them marked by a radical simplicity of style; and another novel, "A Farewell to Arms", appeared in 1929, even more pessimistic than the first, depicting life as a big trap in which the protagonist is caught.

In the Thirties Hemingway travelled widely through Europe and Africa, and while he was in America he spent most of his time fishing in Key West, Florida. From his frequent stays in Spain a very personal book on bullfighting resulted in 1932, "Death in the Afternoon"; and his African travels led to an autobiographical report on big game hunting in his book "The Green Hills of Africa" (1935).

In 1933, Hemingway published yet another collection of short stories, "Winner Take Nothing", to which he added some new stories in 1938 (among them "The Short Happy Life of Francis Macomber" and "The Snows of Kilimanjaro") when he gathered all his short stories along with his only play under the title "The Fifth Column and the First Forty-Nine".

In 1936 he went to Spain as a war correspondent to report on the Spanish Civil War; he was a supporter of the Republican side. His novel "For Whom the Bell Tolls" (1940) impressively relates an episode from this war.

By 1940 Hemingway had been married and divorced three times. He married again in 1944 and moved to a farm in Cuba. However, during World War II Hemingway was in Europe again, this time with the US army.

After World War II Hemingway did not write much any more; he dedicated a lot of time to hunting in Africa, survived two plane crashes and lived a withdrawn, "natural" life. However, in 1952 he published one more book, his last; the story of "The Old Man and the Sea". This story was to become his greatest success. E. Hemingway was awarded the Nobel Prize in 1954.

Hemingway died from his own hand in Ketchum, Idaho, on July 2, 1961, as the result of an "accident"; when cleaning his rifle, he fired a bullet through his head.

Reaktionen, Gedanken und Einstellungen entfalten können. Wenn die Klasse interessiert und im Lesen geübt ist, und der Lehrer mit seinem literarischen Text nicht nur gut vertraut ist, sondern seine Schüler auch entsprechend zu motivieren vermag, kann es durchaus sein, daß schließlich die Ergebnisse des im Unterricht gemeinsam Erarbeiteten den Abstand zwischen „schulischer" und „akademischer" Textinterpretation gering erscheinen lassen.

Im folgenden sollen einige wichtige methodische Voraussetzungen für erfolgreiche Textarbeit in den Klassen 10 und 11 genannt werden.

☐ Längere literarische Texte, vor allem Romane, erlauben extensives Lesen; die kursorische Behandlung längerer Passagen wechselt ab mit der statarischen Durchnahme von Schlüsselstellen, oder aber der Text wird von bestimmten „Plateaus" aus in größeren Zusammenhängen besprochen. Die meisten Kurzgeschichten hingegen verlangen wegen ihrer starken erzählerischen Konzentration grundsätzlich die intensive, schrittweise fortschreitende Besprechung. In vielen Fällen werden die Schüler die Short Story zunächst einmal ganz lesen; die Durchnahme jedoch wird in inhaltlich sinnvollen Abschnitten erfolgen (z. B. Episoden, die „szenisch" in sich geschlossen sind). Entsprechend wird die häusliche Vorbereitung in der schrittweisen sprachlichen und inhaltlichen Klärung dieser Textabschnitte bestehen.

☐ Erst wenn die sprachlichen Schwierigkeiten geklärt sind, kann ein literarischer Text mit Verständnis gelesen werden.

Gewissenhafte häusliche Vorbereitung des zu erarbeitenden Textes ist daher unverzichtbar. Schüler, die ihren Text nicht kennen, hemmen den Unterrichtsablauf. Der Lehrer muß deshalb die häusliche Vorbereitung der Schüler gezielt überprüfen.

☐ Schüler müssen – zumal in der 10. und 11. Klasse – konzentriertes Lesen erst lernen. Dies gilt sowohl für das *reading for gist* als auch für das *reading for detail*. Aus diesem Grunde ist es wichtig, den Schülern zu ihrer Aufgabe der häuslichen Textvorbereitung gezielt Leitfragen mitzugeben, welche ihre Aufmerksamkeit in bestimmte Richtungen lenken.

☐ Der zu besprechende Textteil muß ständig im Unterricht „gegenwärtig" sein; in der Regel sollte er daher im ersten Teil der Stunde (etwa nach einem Wiederholungsgespräch, das die Stunde an die vorangegangene anknüpft) in der Klasse noch einmal gelesen werden. Der Text ist somit Ausgangs- und ständiger Bezugspunkt. Auch sollten die Schüler lernen, sich auf den Text zu beziehen, indem sie daran gewöhnt werden, relevante Passagen zu zitieren. Wenn die Zeit zum Lesen des Textes nicht ausreicht, sollten zumindest einige wichtige Passagen zu gegebener Zeit herausgegriffen und von Schülern vorgetragen werden. (Das abschließende Lesen nach der Besprechung, früher oft als „krönender Abschluß" praktiziert, ist die schwächere Alternative.)

☐ Bevor in der Klasse über einen literarischen Text diskutiert wird, sollte sichergestellt sein, daß er inhaltlich voll verstanden ist. Daher empfiehlt es sich, die Schüler grundsätzlich eine Paraphrase geben zu lassen, bevor es an die Ausdeutung geht. (Meist liefert die Paraphrase

auch den Ansatzpunkt für den Tafelanschrieb.) In vielen Fällen kann die Paraphrase sehr knapp gehalten werden; zuweilen läßt es sich nicht vermeiden, daß Paraphrase und Ausdeutung Hand in Hand gehen.

☐ Für die Textarbeit gilt prinzipiell die Regel: keine Stunde ohne Tafelanschrieb! Die Abfolge der einzelnen Schritte, etwa von der Paraphrase zur Ausdeutung, beziehungsweise die Darstellung von Konfigurationen oder Entwicklungen (verdeutlicht durch Pfeile oder Bezugslinien) sollte zum Schluß der Stunde als Ergebnis gewissermaßen „lesbar" im Tafelanschrieb dastehen. Die Schüler werden daran gewöhnt, sich während des Unterrichts Notizen zu machen und auch jeweils den Tafelanschrieb mitzunotieren.

☐ Im Verlaufe des den Text erschließenden Unterrichtsgesprächs erweitern die Schüler ständig ihr Interpretationsvokabular. Bei geeigneter Gelegenheit, z. B. nach Abschluß der Lektüre einer Kurzgeschichte, sollten die bereits bekannten Begriffe von den Schülern (in Gruppenarbeit) zusammengestellt werden. Das Arbeitsblatt S. 79/80 kann dabei Verwendung finden, selbst wenn die Schüler noch nicht alle aufgeführten und erklärten *literary terms* zu kennen brauchen. (Evtl. Auswahl treffen!) Hierbei könnten durchaus auch verfügbare Hilfen hinzugezogen werden, wie etwa H. O. Hohmann, Englisch diskutieren, Englischdeutscher Diskussionswortschatz mit Satzbeispielen, München, Langenscheidt 1982[2]. Desgleichen könnten Lehrer und Schüler nach der Analyse mehrerer Short Stories gemeinsam einen Interpretationsraster erstellen, der den Schülern bei künftigen eigenen Interpretationsversuchen den methodischen Zugang erleichtern würde. (Vgl. den Vorschlag von

Stockebrand/Nadorf in: Der fremdsprachliche Unterricht, Heft 64, Klett, Stuttgart 1982, S. 304; ferner die Modelle von P. Freese und Brusch/Köhring.)

☐ Um der Monotonie eines methodischen Schematismus zu entgehen, muß sich der Lehrer um Variabilität bemühen. Das bedeutet etwa: Einsatz von Kontrasttexten und Zusatzmaterialien; Schülerreferate; falls möglich und zugänglich Vergleich mit Verfilmungen des Textes (nach der Lektüre!); Mischung von intensiver und extensiver Textarbeit; Ergänzung eines literarischen Textes durch landeskundliche Sachtexte; gelegentliche Gruppenarbeit zu sprachlichen oder stilistischen Untersuchungen; eventuell der Versuch, die Schüler selbst schöpferisch schreiben zu lassen (*creative writing*); usw.

Zur Konzeption des Heftes

Die Stundenblätter sind das Ergebnis wiederholter eigener Unterrichtserfahrungen mit den behandelten Kurzgeschichten Hemingways, und darüber hinaus auch das Resultat exemplarischer Analyse im Studienseminar.

Jedoch sollten Sie sich als Lehrer durch die Stundenentwürfe nicht zu sehr gegängelt fühlen, sondern Ihre Flexibilität behalten. Betrachten Sie die Stundenblätter als Vorschläge, die Varianten keinesfalls ausschließen; fügen Sie hinzu oder lassen Sie fort, wo es Ihnen sinnvoll erscheint. So kann beispielsweise das Durchnahmetempo durchaus variieren; gelegentlich werden Hinweise auf die Möglichkeit einer gerafften Behandlung gegeben. Um dem Eindruck einer zu starken Gängelung zu begegnen, ist des öfteren ein methodisches Vorgehen als Erweiterung

empfohlen (z. B. zur Sprache Hemingways).

Die grundlegenden Unterrichtsziele der Textarbeit im Englischunterricht der Klassen 10 und 11 werden nicht im einzelnen aufgeführt, sondern als bekannt vorausgesetzt. Die eigentlichen Stundenblätter sind in die Spalten „Unterrichtsschritte", „Unterrichtsformen" und „Fragestellungen" gegliedert. Die Spalte „Unterrichtsschritte" läßt Thema, Aufbau und inhaltliche Strukturierung der Stunde deutlich werden. Die Spalte „Unterrichtsformen" liefert stichwortartig methodische Hinweise; im Textteil des Buches sind diese Hinweise in vielen Fällen weiter ausformuliert. (Der Bezeichnung „Unterrichtsgespräch" wurde im allgemeinen der Vorzug vor dem sonst üblichen Begriff „Lehrer-Schüler-Gespräch" (L-S-G) gegeben, um deutlich werden zu lassen, daß im optimalen Unterrichtsgeschehen nicht immer der Lehrer die Schaltstation ist, sondern die Schüler so oft wie möglich direkt aufeinander eingehen.) In der Spalte „Fragestellungen" werden Fragen angeregt, die in dieser Form dazu geeignet sind, die Schüler in angemessener, logisch konsequenter Weise gedanklich zu führen. Prinzipiell stehen paraphrasierende Fragen vor Fragen zur Ausdeutung des Textes. Die Beantwortung der Fragestellungen erfolgt im interpretierenden Teil des Buches, ohne daß die Fragen im einzelnen jeweils aufgegriffen und die Antworten mit Formulierungsvorschlägen versehen werden. Der Bezug der Interpretation zu den Fragestellungen ist jederzeit deutlich erkennbar. Das Schwergewicht der Stundenblätter wurde auf den Tafelanschrieb gelegt, weil dieser für die Sicherung der Ergebnisse von großer Wichtigkeit ist. Natürlich können die Formulierungen verkürzter an die Tafel oder auf den Tageslichtprojektor geschrieben werden als es hier im Druck aus Gründen der Verständlichkeit geschieht.

Die Zweisprachigkeit des Buchteils entspricht den von manchen Kollegen geäußerten Wünschen und Bedürfnissen des Praktikers: was sich auf die methodisch-didaktische Organisation des Unterrichts bezieht, ist auf Deutsch verfaßt; hingegen ist der größere, interpretatorische Teil in der Ziel- und Unterrichtssprache Englisch geschrieben.

Indian Camp

Hemingways Kurzgeschichte „Indian Camp" wird aus gutem Grund häufig im Englischunterricht gelesen. Sie ist sprachlich ohne weiteres von Schülern am Ende der Sekundarstufe I oder am Anfang der Sekundarstufe II zu bewältigen, hat einen fesselnden Inhalt und ist wie aus einem Guß gestaltet. An „Indian Camp" lassen sich vorzüglich charakteristische Merkmale einer Short Story erarbeiten (wie *open beginning* und *open ending;* straffe Ökonomie im Gesamten, Konzentration auf wesentliche Situationen, Beschränkung auf wenige Personen, Knappheit der Darstellung, Reduktion und äußerste Verdichtung im Sprachlichen, etc.). Auch was die Erzähltechnik anbelangt, ist die Geschichte interessant, da Hemingway Stilmittel aus der Filmtechnik übernimmt, indem er häufig drastische Schnitte macht, die den Leser abrupt von einer Situation in die nächste versetzen. Darüber hinaus eignet sich „Indian Camp" besonders als Einstieg in die Behandlung von *initiation stories*.

Auf nur vier Seiten wird ein prägnantes Erlebnis geschildert, das mit der nächtlichen Fahrt über einen nebelverhangenen See einsetzt und mit der zum Anfang korrespondierenden Rückfahrt über den See bei Tagesanbruch endet. Wegen des unvermittelten Beginns der Kurzgeschichte wird nicht sogleich klar, wer die erwähnten Personen sind, woher sie kommen und wohin sie unterwegs sind. Erst allmählich, im Gespräch, durch nachträglich, sozusagen versetzt gelieferte Informationen erfährt der Leser Einzelheiten, wenn auch nicht erschöpfend. Manches muß vom Leser selber erschlossen werden. Offenbar haben zwei junge Indianer mitten in der Nacht Nicks Vater, einen Arzt (dessen Nachnamen wir nicht erfahren) aufgesucht und ihn gebeten, sofort zum Indianerlager im Wald jenseits des Sees mitzukommen, um dort einer Indianerin zu helfen, bei der sich eine Geburtskomplikation eingestellt hat. Da sich später herausstellt, daß der Arzt nur Jagdmesser und Fischfangutensilien, jedoch keine geeigneten Instrumente und auch kein Betäubungsmittel bei sich hat, liegt die Vermutung nahe, daß die Indianer ihn in einem Lager oder in einer Jagdhütte aufgefunden haben. Das würde auch erklären, warum „Uncle George" ihn begleitet und warum er seinen Sohn Nick mitnimmt, der nicht älter als etwa 10 Jahre sein dürfte, und den er vielleicht nicht allein zurücklassen wollte.

Dieser kleine Nick wird nun unvermittelt Zeuge zweier blutiger Erlebnisse, die in ihrer Intensität mehr sind, als ein Bub seines Alters normalerweise verkraften kann. Nach der Ankunft der Männer im Indianerlager muß er seinem Vater eine Schale halten, als dieser – wie sich für den Leser erst im nachhinein herausstellt – mit primitivsten Mitteln und ohne Betäubung eine Kaiserschnittoperation durchführt. Nick versucht nicht hinzuschauen; aber da ist noch das furchtbare, quälende Schreien der jungen Indianerin, von dem sein Vater sagt, es sei nicht wichtig... Die unbeschreibliche Operation dauert lange. Dann ist das Baby (ein Junge!) endlich geboren, und alle Beteiligten atmen erleichtert auf. Als Nicks Vater sich nun um den Mann der jungen Mutter kümmern will, wird Nick ein weiteres Mal Zeuge einer schockierenden Szene. In grausamer Deutlichkeit sieht er, wie sein Vater die Decke vom halbabgetrennten Kopf des jungen Indianers fortzieht. Der Mann hat die qualvolle Operation an seiner Frau nicht ertragen können und sich die Kehle durchgeschnitten. So erlebt Nick unvermittelt nebeneinander Geburt und Tod, beide in extremer Gestalt. Der Schmerz, der von der jungen Mutter zu erleiden war, und das Blut, das vergossen wurde, um einem kleinen Jungen das Leben zu schenken, bedeuten einen fast unerträglichen Eindruck für Nick; der beinahe gleichzeitig sich ereignende Selbstmord, der entsetzliche Anblick des Bluts, des unverhofften Todes, kommen für Nick als weiterer Schock hinzu, dessen Wirkung sich nur ahnen läßt.

Als Nick – diesmal allein mit seinem Vater – auf dem Heimweg ist, gehen die Bilder der Nacht durch seinen Kopf, hat er viele Fragen. Später aber, im Boot, das sein Vater rudert, ist der Bub der festen Überzeugung, daß er nie sterben wird!

Zum methodischen Vorgehen

Um die Wirkung dieser Kurzgeschichte voll zu entfalten, sollte „Indian Camp" ohne Unterbrechung gelesen werden.

Hausaufgabe für die 1. Stunde: Die Schüler sollen die Kurzgeschichte ganz durchlesen und auf sich wirken lassen. Sodann schlagen sie entweder in den *annotations* oder in einem einsprachigen Wörterbuch die beim Lesen unterstrichenen unbekannten Vokabeln nach und notieren sie auf einem separaten Bogen in der Reihenfolge ihres Erscheinens im Text. („Indian Camp" enthält etwa 30 den Schülern unbekannte Wörter, von denen jedoch fast die Hälfte aus dem Kontext heraus verständlich wird.) Alsdann lesen sie die Short Story ein zweites Mal ganz. Als begleitende Aufgabenstellung notieren die Schüler sich Möglichkeiten einer Gliederung der Kurzgeschichte.

Es wäre auch denkbar, bereits bei der Aufgabenstellung einige für das Verständnis der Geschichte wichtige Begriffe zu klären (z. B. Wörter aus dem Umfeld *childbirth: labour pains, Caesarian, anaesthetic, incision, pero-*

xide, interne, etc.), oder in einem Informationsgespräch den Hintergrund der Geschichte etwas zu verdeutlichen (z. B. hinsichtlich solcher *Indian camps* wie des in der Short Story erwähnten der *bark-peelers*). Natürlich können derartige sachlichen Klärungen auch ohne weiteres zu Beginn der folgenden Stunde während der Besprechung des ersten Teils der Kurzgeschichte miteinfließen.

Am Anfang der Behandlung von Hemingways „Indian Camp" steht nach einer knappen inhaltlichen Zusammenfassung der Kurzgeschichte durch einen oder mehrere Schüler die Textgliederung in drei größere Abschnitte, deren mittlerer sich wiederum dreifach gliedern läßt, so daß eine Untergliederung in insgesamt fünf Teile möglich ist. Diese fünf Abschnitte werden in vier Unterrichtsstunden schrittweise besprochen. Jede Stunde steht unter einem zentralen Thema. Es wäre wünschenswert, für den mittleren Hauptteil der Geschichte eine Doppelstunde zur Verfügung zu haben.

Da Hemingway in dieser Geschichte die Technik abrupter „Schnitte" verwendet, wie sie von Filmen her bekannt ist, muß beim Lesen vor allem auch auf die Wirkung solcher unvermittelter Übergänge geachtet werden. Weil vieles Wichtige ungesagt bleibt, ausgespart wird, muß die Aufmerksamkeit des Lesers mancherlei Informationen selber erschließend bereitstellen. Aus diesem Grunde ist die genaue Paraphrase bei der schrittweise vorgehenden Besprechung von „Indian Camp" besonders wichtig.

Alternativvorschlag:

Gemeinsames Erarbeiten des ersten Teils der Kurzgeschichte (Exposition) in der Klasse. Die Schüler lesen dann den Rest der Geschichte zu Hause, gliedern sie, schlagen unbekannte Vokabeln nach, lesen nochmals und beantworten Leitfragen.

Übersicht über die Unterrichtseinheit „Indian Camp"

Stunde	Zentrales Stundenthema	Textgliederung	Textstellen
1	The Exposition	I Getting to the Indian Camp	from the beginning up to: ...holding a lamp.
2	The Caesarian Operation in the Indian Shanty	II a) Preparing the Operation	from: Inside on a wooden bunk... up to: ..."I'd rather not touch it."
		b) The Operation	from: Later when he started to operate... up to: ...Nick put the basin out in the kitchen.
3	The Two Fathers	c) The Discovery of the Young Indian Father's Suicide	from: Uncle George looked at his arm... up to: ...tipped the Indians's head back.
4	The Result of Nick's Experience	III Returning from the Indian Camp	from: It was just beginning to be daylight... to the end.

1. Stunde:
Getting to the Indian Camp

Unterrichtsschritt 1:
Hinführung zur Short Story „Indian Camp"

Falls nicht bereits in einem vorbereitenden Gespräch zum Ende der vorangegangenen Stunde erfolgt (= Zeitersparnis, die der Besprechung des ersten Teils zugute käme!), würde ein Einstieg über die gegenwärtigen Lebensumstände der Indianer Nordamerikas rasch den Brückenschlag zurück zum Anfang dieses Jahrhunderts ermöglichen. Allerdings ist es nicht notwendig, an dieser Stelle ausführlich über die Geschichte der Indianer Nordamerikas zu diskutieren, denn es geht in Hemingways Short Story nicht um die Indianerproblematik, sondern um Grunder-fahrungen menschlicher Existenz, um menschliche Verhaltensweisen angesichts des Leidens und des Todes. (Warum es aber doch nicht zufällig gerade ein Indianerlager ist. in dem Nick Zeuge von Geburt und Tod wird, soll erst später besprochen werden, vgl. S. 29).

Die Diskussion des Unterrichtsschrittes 1 sollte etwa zu folgenden Ergebnissen führen: Nowadays most North American Indians live on reservations allotted to them by the US government. "For nearly 300 years, the relations between whites and Indians were a succession of misunderstandings, broken treaties and massacres. Finally, the whites took possession of almost the whole country, and the surviving Indians were herded onto reservations. Until the 20th century these reservations resembled vast ghettos, and it is only since 1934 that they have developed into a means for the preservation of half-shattered cultures." (I. Friebel / H. Händel [eds.]: Britain – USA Now. A Survey in Key Words, Frankfurt [4]1979, p. 106) These reservations are not identical with "camps" such as the one described in the short story. Indian camps are usually mobile camps which are put up at harvest time when skill is particularly in demand. Indians are employed by the whites to do the type of work that they are better qualified for due to their traditionally more nature-oriented life-styles and, of course, they also provide a cheap labour force! (In our time the natural capacity of Indians for working at a great height without fear of dizziness has led to the almost exclusive employment of Indians in the construction of sky-scrapers!) The bark-peelers' job consisted in removing the bark from felled trees while they were still in the forest. The Indians worked for and were paid by whites, but they lived in their own small camping communities. When medical help was urgently needed they had to send for a white doctor from the nearest settlement or town.

Um das Interesse der Schüler an der Geschichte nicht durch typisch „lehrerhafte" Vokabelkontrolle wieder zu dämpfen, empfiehlt es sich, das Gespräch über die Camps und die gelegentliche Notwendigkeit ärztlicher Hilfe für die Indianer in solchen Lagern unaufdringlich zu dem spezifischen Beispiel einer Geburtenkomplikation hinzulenken, so daß sich die Fragen nach Wörtern wie *labour pain, Caesarian, an anaesthetic, pre- and postoperative, incision* usw. ganz organisch ergeben.

Unterrichtsschritt 2:
Knappe Inhaltsangabe der Kurzgeschichte

Bei der kurzen Inhaltsangabe sollen die Schüler nur die wesentlichen Fakten referieren.

Unterrichtsschritt 3:
Gliederung der Kurzgeschichte

Unter Einbezug der Hausaufgabe unterteilen die Schüler Hemingways Short Story zunächst in drei größere Abschnitte, dann genauer in insgesamt fünf Abschnitte, da der mittlere Hauptteil zwei deutliche Einschnitte aufweist. Die von den Schülern vorgeschlagenen Überschriften zu den jeweiligen Abschnitten werden im Tafelanschrieb notiert. (→ T 1)

Unterrichtsschritt 4:
The Exposition

A student reads out the beginning of the short story up to "Oh, said Nick." As there is a cut between this line and the next ("Across the bay they found...") it seems feasible to discuss the "setting" (the place and time in which the action takes place; the environment of the characters) and the persons mentioned, before reading and paraphrasing the rest of the introductory part.
The students will be struck by the abruptness of the opening of the story: "At the lake shore..." (which lake? which lake shore?) "... there was another rowboat drawn up." ("another" implies that one boat – not specifically mentioned – must be there already.) "The two Indians stood waiting." (What Indians? Waiting for whom and for what purpose?) "Nick and his father..." (Who are they? What's their last name? Where do they come from? What do they look like? Why has Nick's father decided to take his son with him?) "Uncle George sat in the stern..." (Who is he? What has he got to do with the others? Were the three camping out together?) The reader is kept guessing.
Obviously, though, Nick, the young boy, must be of special importance in this story, as the two adults, his relatives, are constantly referred to as "Nick's father" and

(Nick's) "Uncle George". Their last names seem to be irrelevant; relevant, however, is their relation to the boy.

How, then, does Hemingway's short story "Indian Camp" open? We are "right into it", receive a minimum of information, only the bare outlines of a situation and of a handful of persons.

This kind of opening of a short story can be called an "open beginning". What actual information we get refers to factual description, such as the rowboats, and the position of the passengers in the boat. (Uncle George in the stern of the camp rowboat, Nick and his father in the stern of the other Indian's boat. (→ T2) Maybe the students will notice that one short sentence goes slightly beyond factual description, and adds a sudden touch of emotion to the otherwise rather unemotional scene: "Nick lay back with his father's arm around him." What does this line reveal about the relationship between father and son? It is obviously one of trust; the boy feels safe and protected within his father's arm. Nick calls his father "Dad". He must be a very young boy, since, for example, he asks his father only now, when they are well on their way, about the purpose of their journey. His father, on the other hand, seems to be fond enough of his boy to take him with him on an adventurous excursion such as this one. (But then we don't really know, maybe he just couldn't leave Nick behind all by himself.)

Is there anything else we can say about Nick's father at this point? In answer to his son's question when he tells him their destination, the Indian camp, Nick's father adds that "an Indian lady" is very sick. The word "lady" is surprising here, it stands out somehow. What word would we have expected instead? "An Indian woman", or "a squaw" perhaps. What does the choice of the formal word "lady" reveal about the speaker? Maybe it is just the polite way in which a parent talking to a child would refer to a woman. But it also shows that he respects the Indians, that he doesn't look down on them and that he wants his son to be well aware of this.

This could be considered an indirect characterisation of Nick's father. When called upon to help a human being in distress, even in the middle of the night, the white doctor does not hesitate to set out. Without considering for a moment the colour of his patient's skin, he displays a natural, matter-of-fact willingness to do his job as a doctor. Nick's father's determination as well as his reassuring protective gesture create an impression of strength and security. On the other hand, Nick's cuddling into his father's arm accentuates the contrast with the uncanny nightly atmosphere around them. Darkness, mist on the water, the cold night air: Hemingway suggests, rather than describes, an atmosphere of uncertainty, hostility even. This is underlined by the silence of the men. The silence is broken only once, by Nick's natural (but also symbolic) question "Where are we going, Dad?" The eeriness of the nightly crossing in mist and darkness may have prompted this (slightly fearful?) question. The reader senses this ambivalent atmosphere that leaves him with vague outlines only, keeps him guessing.

After this detailed analysis of the opening of the short story a student should read the rest of the introductory part (from "Across the bay..." up to "An old woman stood in the doorway holding a lamp.") which can be discussed more quickly.

In the second part of the opening passage the men's journey from the lake to the camp is described briefly, but realistically: their way through a soaking wet meadow, into the woods, a trail, then a logging road until they get to the camp.

Again, it is worthwhile considering the atmosphere of this nightly excursion: the red shimmer of Uncle George's cigar lighting up in the dark from time to time, the shine of the young Indian's lantern barely penetrating the mist and darkness over the wet meadow, then later on the faint light on the logging road and, finally, the light in the shanty window and the lamp in the old woman's hand. All these variations in shades of darkness lit up only occasionally and partly by restricted light sources, contribute to a sense of uncertainty and insecurity. The men cannot see clearly. The dog that comes barking at them adds an element of hostility.

We wonder what scene is going to unfold behind the doorway when the men enter the shanty.

The abrupt opening of this short story, the scant description of the setting, the bare character outlines, the implicit suggestion of a very specific atmosphere: all of these elements combine to form the exposition of Hemingway's "Indian Camp".

It may seem too soon to say something about Hemingway's style at this point. However, the students will have been alerted to the fact that behind the author's "simple", realistic, curt language there are hidden meanings and suggestions which the reader should try to grasp.

Hausaufgabe:

Die Schüler sollen „Indian Camp" noch einmal lesen; durch die Leitfragen wird ihre Aufmerksamkeit vor allem auf das Verhalten Nicks und der beiden Väter vor und während der Operation gelenkt.

2. Stunde:
The Caesarian Operation

Unterrichtsschritt 1:
Wiederholung der Ergebnisse

The students recapitulate briefly what they found out about the "setting", "persons", and "atmosphere" in the previous lesson; they may refer to their notes, but should use their own words.

The effect of the opening passages of the short story on the reader is complex and confusing: the reader – like Nick – does not see clearly yet. It is the function of the first part of the story which we have characterized as "exposition", to arouse our curiosity for what follows, and to focus our attention on the central experience of this story.

Unterrichtsschritt 2:
Preparing for the Operation

The text should be read out from "Inside on a wooden bunk..." to ... "I'd rather not touch it"; it should then be paraphrased by the students, and interpreted.

The situation inside the shanty is seen from the door through which Nick's father and Uncle George are the first to enter, followed by Nick and the two Indians. A young Indian woman in the lower bunk of a bunk bed has been in labour pains for two days. With her are old women from the camp. But all the wisdom and experience of the old women cannot help the young expectant mother in her suffering. How terrible her pain must have been can be read between the lines: the men in the camp have moved away from this shanty, up the road "to sit in the dark and (to) smoke out of the range of the noise she made"! The noise, i.e. the young woman's screams, is so heart-rending that the Indian men attempt to escape from it! (Now we see why they sent for the doctor, and understand the haste of the young Indian rowers.)

How must Nick feel when he enters the shanty and just at that moment is exposed to one of those dreadful, painful screams? Those tough Indian men have moved "out of the range" of these screams, but poor Nick has to be directly confronted with them!

How nervous, how confused he must feel! The young woman's husband is lying in the upper bunk. What do we learn about him? He, obviously, has not run away from his wife's screams. But then he is in pain himself, as he has cut his foot "badly with an axe". This was three days ago. A skillful Indian bark-peeler who cuts his foot with an axe? A surprising fact. But considering that the accident happened the day before his wife started to be in labour, it casts a revealing light on the young man's state of nerves. He was probably nervous with anticipation, thinking of his pregnant wife, the impending birth, the baby – so his axe slipped... And why is he smoking in his upper bunk now, filling the whole room with the reek of his tobacco? Most likely for the same reason: he must be extremely nervous and terse, with his wife suffering and screaming directly underneath him.

How, on the other hand, can we characterize Nick's father's reaction to the situation? The moment he enters the shanty he seems to be in control of the situation. He wants boiling water (to sterilize his instruments), he explains to Nick what has to be done in situations such as this one, and all in all responds just as a doctor should. Beginning to explain the situation to his son he becomes quite factual; Nick's perfunctory, automatic "I know" is firmly rebuked by a stern, determined "You don't know. Listen to me." And he goes on to explain to the boy in simple, easily intelligible sentences what "being in labour" means, and why a woman in labour screams. Nick understands. "I see." – But just then the woman screams again, and Nick's immediate, spontaneous reaction shows that all his father's rational, down-to-earth explanations cannot wipe out his feeling of sympathy with the woman who is suffering such pain. "Oh, Daddy, can't you give her something to make her stop screaming?" We feel the intensity of Nick's plea in his appealing "Oh, Daddy".

However, his "Daddy" can't stop the woman's pain as he hasn't got any anaesthetic with him. Instead he tries to convince Nick that the woman's screams are "not important" to him as a doctor. In fact he doesn't really take any notice of them. "I don't hear them because they are not important." Labour pain, to him, is part of the natural process of birth. What attitude can we discern behind the doctor's words? Is Nick's father a cold and heartless man without any sympathy with his suffering patient? Has he become hardened by his profession over the years? Or is he concentrating so much on this patient's specific case that he knows he cannot afford any distraction? At any rate, when he makes the remark about the woman's painful screams not being important, Hemingway accentuates this by mentioning that the husband in the upper bunk (who keeps hearing his wife's tortured screaming) rolls over against the wall... A suggestion perhaps, that what's "not important" to the doctor may be of utmost importance to the young husband, just as it is bound to affect Nick.

The boy sees his father unwrapping "several things" from his handkerchief without bothering to investigate what they are; and the doctor continues explaining to his son what problems can arise if there are complications in the birth process. All this while Nick keeps watching his father's hands. The doctor's conclusion: "Maybe we'll have to operate on this lady" is again followed by a reference to his hands. The doctor's hands become the focal point of his medical skill, when he "goes to work". Nick's father has now become a concentrated surgeon, entirely intent on the operation he is about to perform.

Unterrichtsschritt 3:
The Operation

The students read the text out from "Later when he started to operate..." to "Nick put the basin out in the kitchen", then paraphrase and interpret it.

Surprisingly, the actual operation itself is presented in very few lines; it is not described in any detail whatsoever. These lines, however, provide an excellent opportunity for students to note a great number of facts that are not explicitly stated in the text, but are to be inferred by the reader. An exercise in reading between, or rather, behind the lines.

The paragraph begins rather abruptly: "Later, when he started to operate..." There is no immediate link with the doctor's previous statement: "maybe we'll have to operate"; Hemingway leaves out completely the result of the doctor's examination and his subsequent decision to operate. The reader must fill in the missing information himself and realize that obviously the doctor had no other choice but to operate.

"... Uncle George and three Indian men held the woman still." What Hemingway does not explicitly say is why four strong men are needed to hold the woman still during the operation. Again the reader must fill in the missing information himself, remembering the doctor's earlier comment "I haven't any anaesthetic". The young woman is undergoing an operation without any pain-killer! Moreover, what sort of operation is this? We do not learn this until afterwards: a Caesarian, i. e. an operation in which the surgeon must cut open the mother's womb. The reader can imagine the

unspeakable pain, the extreme suffering the woman experiences! No wonder that four men have to hold her down.

What else is not said? We learn afterwards what "instruments" the doctor is forced to use (jack-knife and tapered gut-leaders = hunting and fishing instruments! We can conclude then that – as the doctor has neither anaesthetic nor any proper instruments with him – he, his son and Uncle George must have been out camping when the Indians fetched them.)

Hemingway writes only that the woman bites Uncle George in the arm and Uncle George instinctively starts swearing "damn squaw bitch" – without meaning any offence, as the young Indian's laughing response seems to prove. The Indian's laughter almost distracts us from the fact that the woman behaves like a tortured animal. "Nick held the basin for his father." This sentence brings Nick back into the picture: all this time Nick has been right in the middle of it all as an eyewitness. Whether the boy likes it or not, he's got to assist in the operation by holding the basin with the "instruments". And ... "it all took a long time"! The last sentence of this brief paragraph underlines the horror of the crude Caesarian operation, whose impact on the boy we can, at best, infer. Avoiding naturalistic detail, Hemingway manages in the brevity of just five lines to express the essence of a process which in actual fact is painfully and almost unbearably long. Hemingway's technique of leaving certain information out at the time, and handing it to the reader *post festum* has a mitigating effect. The shock comes with delayed action, as it were. The full impact of Hemingway's style is achieved on re-reading the whole story.

"See, it's a boy, Nick." The doctor's words mean a relief, although the operation hasn't come to an end yet. He shows the baby boy to his son, but Nick looks away... Again, the reader has to infer the obvious! The sight of blood that his father is used to as a doctor, and of the open wound (womb) are too much for Nick. And when his father puts "something" in the basin (the afterbirth!) commenting "There. That gets it.", Nick again doesn't look at the basin he is holding. And there is a third time, when his father is sewing up the incision he has made, that Nick looks away. What conclusion can we draw from Nick's behaviour? This night's experience must have shaken the young boy to the core. How relieved must Nick feel when his father, at long last, has finished and Nick can put the basin down in the kitchen, out of sight!

3. Stunde:
The Two Fathers

Unterrichtsschritt 1:
Kurze Wiederholung der Ergebnisse

Falls keine Doppelstunde zur Verfügung steht, muß zunächst an die vorangegangene Stunde angeknüpft werden.

Unterrichtsschritt 2:
The Discovery of the Young Indian Father's Suicide

The students read the text out from "Uncle George looked at his arm . . ." to ". . . tipped the Indian's head back", then – after a brief paraphrase – discuss this passage.

When the operation is over at long last, Nick's father, too, is relieved. But for a while he is still quite "the doctor": he notices Uncle George looking at his arm and the young Indian's reminiscent smile (remembering the bite and Uncle George's "damn squaw bitch"!) and decides to put some peroxide on the wound; then he has another close look at his patient, the young

mother, and finally makes a few comments on further proceedings. Maybe the students will notice that Nick's father is suddenly called "the doctor" here, thus stressing the totally professional attitude he displays at this point. The comparison with the exaltation and talkativeness of football players after a game stresses this professional aspect, too.

After the medical problems have been seen to the doctor unwinds and becomes talkative. It is only now that the reader is confronted with the full impact of the primitiveness of the Caesarian operation when he learns from the doctor's words with what crude means the operation has been performed. But how does the doctor talk about his success? "That's one for the medical journal", he says. Is this bragging, showing off, the expression of vanity? Or do his words contain a certain amount of self-irony, of ironical distance between the speaker and what he says? What do we make of Uncle George's comment on the doctor's words then? (Is there possibly some slight depreciation in his voice?) In Uncle George's "Oh, you're a great man, all right" the "oh" and the "all right" mark the statement fairly clearly as ironical. If the doctor's tone of voice in this conversation can be imagined as being just as casual as Uncle George's, there wouldn't be any need to characterize Nick's father as "arrogant, vain, conceited, boastful". Naturally, he feels happy after the success of his operation under such miserable, primitive circumstances; he feels elated, even "exalted". Maybe that is why he gets carried away a little when, remembering the "proud father" (here he starts using worn phrases!) he generalizes and plays down the enormity of such operations as the one just performed to "these little affairs" – which does, indeed, sound rather conceited and arrogant.

As a doctor he knows from experience that young fathers are usually "the worst sufferers", and for that reason he feels that he "ought to have a look at the proud father". It also strikes him now that "he took it all pretty quietly." "It all" – the reader remembers what is meant by that; and also that "it all" took a long time ... At this point the doctor appears so confident, so superior to the situation, even more so than before. He seems to know it all: the relativity of pain and suffering, what a woman in labour goes through, and what her husband suffers, too. And then; the anti-climax! What a shocking contrast! In drastic naturalistic detail Hemingway makes sure of the full impact on the reader. Every word in this paragraph is direct description, nothing is left unsaid. While in the previous passages of the story Hemingway left most details to the imagination of the reader (e. g. the word 'blood' is not mentioned once during the operation) and supplied vital information only afterwards (e. g. the instruments used in the operation), the author in this passage indulges in cruel, bloody detail, even mentioning the open razor with which the Indian has cut his throat from ear to ear.

If we compare the doctor's words just before the discovery of the young Indian father's suicide to the reality he is confronted with immediately afterwards, we realize the *dramatic irony* of the situation.

The doctor's words are suddenly revealed as having been unintentionally ambiguous: the "proud" father was indeed "the worst sufferer"! However, it was no "little affair" but a matter of life and death, and he took it all "very quietly", because he couldn't stand witnessing his wife's pain any longer and "quietened" himself for good, i. e. killed himself, quietly, without anyone noticing, with his razor. Possibly the students remember the doctor saying "I don't hear (her screams) because they are not important", and – almost in response – how the Indian husband in the upper bank rolled over against the wall. What is of no import-

ance to the doctor at that moment, is a source of the utmost and ultimately unbearable suffering to the Indian, who has now been discovered dead, "his face toward the wall" (!), in his bunk.

Unterrichtsschritt 3:
The Two Fathers

It is well worthwhile concentrating for a moment on the two fathers, i. e. Nick's dad and the Indian husband. Looking back over the whole scene in the shanty, we see Nick's father as the competent, efficient doctor from the start. He is in control of the situation, doesn't mind the woman's screams, does his work and is rewarded with success. ˙(→ T 5) The Indian husband, however, is hardly mentioned at all. All we know is that he is smoking, he must be nervous, he moves in his bunk ... he commits suicide. (→ T 5)

Paradoxically, success corresponds to suicide (dramatic irony); and there are further correspondences: the "incision" the doctor has made corresponds the Indian's cut throat, the doctor's jackknife corresponds the Indian's razor, "one for the medical journal" "an awful mess", the doctor's pride "the proud father". All this can be made clear in the board diagram. (→ T 5)

The young Indian's razor is sharper than the doctor's hunting knife, and the Indian dies without any noise, while his wife is screaming in tortured pain under the doctor's knife. Must we say, then, that the young Indian father's death is an ironical, or even sarcastic comment on Nick's father's seemingly superior way of handling the situation?

While the doctor is concentrating on saving the mother's (and her baby's) life in a daring, expertly performed operation, he doesn't realize that right above his head there is another life literally on the razor's edge. For all his professionality and skill he does not manage to prevent the Indian's suicide. Could he have prevented it? How? Perhaps if he had not only displayed his medical concern for his patient, but also some human concern for those around him. If he had not only – as an afterthought – demonstrated his experience as a doctor by lightheartedly referring to the young husbands who usually suffer with their wives, but if he had taken this knowledge into consideration before starting on his life-or-death operation, he might have talked to the young Indian, or sent him out of the shanty. Can we discern, then, a certain insensitivity, a lack of human understanding on the part of Nick's father? Doesn't he show a similar lack of empathy with regard to Nick, his young son? Is it not surprising to begin with, that he should take the boy with him on such an excursion in the middle of the night? And then to let Nick witness the whole cruel procedure of the operation, even to let him hold the basin? Does the doctor not consider the consequences that such an experience might have on a child?

Nick's father, this tower of strength, on close scrutiny seems to have flaws, becomes open to criticism.

Hemingway presents (and contrasts) two fathers, the white doctor and the Red Indian, whose lives meet in one momentous situation, – and both have sons. The baby boy is the central cause of his mother's (and father's!) pain and is the reason for the operation (and ultimately for his father's suicide). Nick, on the other hand, has stood by his father's side through this night of almost intolerable extremes: the high tension of the operation, the relief after its seemingly successful completion, the doctor's natural display of pride, and then the Indian's suicide. Not only was Nick forced to be an eye-witness of the Caesarian operation, but he has witnessed, from the kitchen door, every horrible detail of the discovery of the suicide, too. We can only guess what effect this last dreadful experience might

have on the boy. Hemingway makes no comment.

Instead, there is another of those abrupt "cuts".

Hausaufgabe:

Die Schüler sollen sich um eine Deutung des Endes der Kurzgeschichte bemühen. (Leitfragen siehe Stundenblatt)

4. Stunde:
The Result of Nick's Experience

Unterrichtsschritt 1:
Anknüpfen an die vorangegangene Stunde

Die Schüler sollen mit ihrer Zusammenfassung zeigen, daß sie die wesentlichen Pointierungen der auf die Operation folgenden Szene verstanden haben.

Unterrichtsschritt 2:
The Return from the Indian Camp

After the students have read out the final part of the short story from "It was just beginning to be daylight . . .", the discussion will concentrate on the end of Hemingway's "Indian Camp".

The last impression of the nightly scene in the Indian shanty (Nick's father, the lamp in one hand, tipping the Indian's head back) is followed – without transition – by a different scene: The men's return journey in early daylight. The farewell – if there has been any – is not described. The ensuing dialogue between father and son, uninterrupted by any prose comment, seems to be their first conversation after the discovery of the suicide.

Nick's father starts the conversation. He sounds quite different from before, now that his "exhilaration" is gone. In fact, he

25

apologizes to his son for bringing him along on this excursion ("I'm terribly sorry . . ."), and for once calls him "Nickie", a noticeable sign of endearment and closeness. And he adds: "It was an awful mess to put you through."

Remembering what we have already said about Nick's father, this is a remarkable statement. It shows the sort of consideration and insight that seemed to be lacking in him before. Has the doctor perhaps learned a lesson? Has he come to realize that pride comes before a fall, that the moment of his success has in fact turned into a moment of failure for him, with the Indian husband's suicide? Has the coincidence of success and failure made him more aware of his own human limitations? In the course of the night he has had to experience the old wisdom of the Greek tragedians that he who acts must suffer, the tragic paradox that human greatness and human insufficiency are closely interwoven. Can we therefore say that Nick's father comes out of this night as a more understanding, more considerate, perhaps even wiser man?

Nick's response to his father's apology is a battery of questions which proves how very much the two elemental experiences of the night are still alive in the boy's mind. "Do ladies (!) always have such a hard time having babies?", and, abruptly following this first question, "Why did he kill himself, Daddy?" (We note that Nick, too, maintains a high level of intimacy and closeness in this dialogue by calling his father "Daddy" all the time.) The pictures of the night, the almost simultaneous confrontation with the pain of birth and the horror of death (both of them marked out by blood) must have affected the boy deeply.

For once, Nick's "why?" does not receive a clear-cut answer. His father, who seemed to know all the answers before, now admits: "I don't know, Nick." He can only guess. We recall the moment when the doctor rebuked

Nick for perfunctorily saying "I know" stating sharply: "You don't know. Listen." At that point he was so confident and superior! But now his self-confidence is much reduced, and it is obvious that the doctor doesn't know enough about human nature and its guiding principles.

One of Nick's further questions refers to Uncle George. Nick has noticed that Uncle George has absented himself. His question alerts the reader (once again!) to fill in the missing information for himself: Uncle George must have wanted to be alone for a while after that horrible bloody scene in the upper bunk! Even *his* nerves are not strong enough to stomach so much. (We might also assume that his behaviour implies a slight rebuke for Nick's father as well.) Nick seems to sense this. His last question, "Is dying hard, Daddy?", naive as it sounds, shows that his mind is still, and probably will be for some time, full of the scenes of that night. His father's reassuring answer, "No. I think it's pretty easy, Nick. It all depends." does not sound convincing (remembering the open razor and the bloody mess in the bunk bed) and is too vague to have any effect on the boy. Nick cannot yet comprehend that under certain circumstances dying can be easier than living.

Unterrichtsschritt 3:
The Result of Nick's Experience

The end of the story is focused entirely on Nick and his father. The final description shows the two in the boat again, corresponding to the opening of the story. But the night is over now, the mist has disappeared, the sun is coming up, and the water feels warm in the chill of the early morning. Nick sits facing his father, who is rowing. "In the early morning on the lake sitting in the stern of the boat with his father rowing, he felt quite sure that he would never die."

A remarkable last sentence after what Nick

has gone through! What can we say then about the result of Nick's experience?

Nick has taken part in a journey that began in mist and darkness and ends in the light of the early morning sun, a journey touching the extremes of human pain and suffering, human endurance and despair, human courage and skill, human pride and failure. He has been an eye-witness to two central experiences: birth and death, blood shed to give life, and blood shed to take life. We don't know which of the two experiences has shaken him up more. His eyes have been opened to elemental life forces. He tries to look away during the operation "so as not to see what his father was doing", and yet is forced to be right in the middle of it all. In a blunt, unmitigated way Nick has been brought into contact with a part of the adult world which is new and alien, and, indeed, shocking to him. It is an encounter with aspects of a reality that he cannot cope with yet; an initiation that comes too soon for a boy as young as he is. No doubt, he moves one step forward on the long path from childhood to the world of the adults. But the protective padding of childhood is still around him. The events he has witnessed although shaking him thoroughly have not led him to a rational analysis of the situation. In contrast to his father, Nick experiences life entirely on an emotional level. Thus he cannot cope rationally with the events of the night, nor does he grasp that his father's success has been achieved at the expense of some human deficiency. His confidence in his dad is unshaken, there is no critical barrier between them. The last line shows that Nick has not rationalized his experience into some "moral" which he might have learned. On the contrary, the story ends on an optimistic, naive, child-like assertion: with his father rowing Nick feels quite sure that he will never die!

What does this assertion mean?

Unterrichtsschritt 4:
The Meaning of the Last Sentence of the Story

Nick is too young to draw the right conclusions. He is still a child and just as at the opening of the story Nick feels safe within his father's arm, he now has the same want and need of protection. He is sitting opposite his father this time, facing him, however this doesn't mean that he now looks at him in a new light of awareness; he still has the same trust in his father's strength as before. Almost symbolically, the father rows the boat and steers the course, and the son is being rowed, and as yet guided, by his father. Nick is trailing his hand in the water, but typically enough his wet hand does not remind him of his father's hand coming away wet with the Indian's blood, instead he experiences the warmth of the water as a refreshing, promising sensation. (The imagery of water and wetness in this story, which can be traced from the beginning to the end, refers both to life and death.) Of course, Nick is totally unaware of the fact that this picture of his father rowing him in the boat across the water is in itself faintly reminiscent of Charon and the last journey across the river of death in Greek mythology. The young boy sees the bass jumping – a symbol of optimism and the joy of life!

In the early morning light, Nick who is yet in the morning of his life is inclined to suppress the memory of the horrors of the night and in the reassuring nearness of his father clings to that childlike illusion of security and even immortality.

Torn between innocence and experience, Nick still belongs to that paradise of childhood in which "intimations of immortality" (Wordsworth) are possible.

Maybe the students will want to interpret Nick's childish naiveté in the last line as Hemingway's ironical comment on the cruelty and insecurity of human existence as shown in the story. Or perhaps they will want to dismiss it as wishful thinking. Maybe, and this would be a challenging interpretation too, they will tend to interpret the end in psychological terms: Nick's conviction that he will never die could be a typical case of compensation for a sense of insecurity and a deep-rooted fear of death which suddenly besets him as a result of his experience, but is repressed in view of his father's apparent strength.

However the last line is interpreted, it is apparent that in spite of the seemingly optimistic note at the end of the short story, Nick has encountered aspects of human existence that he wasn't aware of before and that have deeply affected him.

In the long run Nick's experience will probably prove to be his very first step towards a recognition of human "reality", and thus a beginning of his initiation into the world of adults. (The literary term "story of initiation" need not be discussed with the class at this point; it will become much more easily intelligible after a discussion of Hemingway's "The Killers" or "The Battler". However, if the students are familiar with the term "initiation", the question might be raised of whether "Indian Camp" can be called an initiation story, and if so, why.)

Unterrichtsschritt 5:
Hemingways Sprache und Stil in
"Indian Camp"

Images and Symbols. Das Herausarbeiten von Bildern und symbolhaften Bezügen soll dazu dienen, die Schüler noch mehr für sprachliche Verdichtungen zu sensibilisieren. Es bietet sich an, die Schüler in Stillarbeit den Text noch einmal durchlesen und alle Stellen kennzeichnen zu lassen, die über ihre konkrete, denotative Bedeutung hinaus möglicherweise eine symbolische Bedeutung haben. (*Wetness: water, blood; light/darkness: lamps, lights, burning cigar, mist, sun,*

etc.) (→ T 7) Es ist auch denkbar, eine derartige sprachliche Untersuchung als Hausaufgabe zu geben, um in der folgenden Stunde mit etwas größerem Zeitaufwand über Hemingways sprachliche Mittel sprechen zu können. (Voraussetzung: Begriffsklärung *symbol, image,* vgl. Arbeitsblatt S. 79.)

Hemingway's Technique of "Cuts". Im Verlaufe der Besprechung von „Indian Camp" ist bereits deutlich geworden, wie knapp, verkürzt, versetzt Hemingway seine Geschichte erzählt. Falls noch nicht geschehen, kann jetzt der Vergleich mit entsprechenden Filmtechniken gezogen werden. Neben der Beschäftigung mit den sprachlichen Mitteln des Autors wird somit den Schülern auch der Einsatz seiner stilistischen Mittel bewußt. Die Schüler sollen erkennen, wie durch Fortlassungen Akzente gesetzt werden können; vor allem jedoch soll deutlich werden, wie damit Leseraktivität geweckt wird.

Diese Stilbetrachtung kann als Hausaufgabe gestellt werden. Die Schüler gehen dreischrittig vor, indem sie beachten a) *what is said,* b) *how it is said,* und c) *what is not said.* Sie formulieren dann selbst die Informationen, die Hemingway bei seinen „cuts" fortgelassen hat.

Unterrichtsabschnitt 6:
Abschließende Bewertung

Zum Abschluß der Besprechung dieser Kurzgeschichte sollte den Schülern Gelegenheit gegeben werden, ihre eigene affektive Betroffenheit erkennen zu lassen. Es empfiehlt sich daher, mit einer offenen Fragestellung zu schließen, um zu sehen, wie die Short Story bei dem Kurs „angekommen" ist und in welcher Richtung die Schüler eventuell selber weiterführende Gedanken entwickeln. Es ist denkbar, daß über eine mögliche Vater-Sohn-Problematik diskutiert wird

(Vorbildcharakter des Vaters, Sich-Lösen vom Vater, Identitätsfindung, usw.). Vielleicht fällt auch auf, daß ausschließlich von Nicks Vater, nie jedoch von seiner Mutter die Rede ist.

(In einer späteren Short Story Hemingways mit dem aufschlußreichen Titel „Fathers and Sons" [1933] blickt der inzwischen 38jährige Nick auf frühere Stationen seines Lebens zurück. Er wird nunmehr selbst von seinem kleinen Sohn befragt, und zwar ausdrücklich auch nach seinem Vater.)

Auch könnte darüber diskutiert werden, warum Hemingway gerade ein *Indian shanty* zum Ort des Geschehens gewählt hat. Ob wohl durch den Fortfall an zivilisatorischer Verkleidung in der natürlichen („primitiven") Umgebung des Indianerlagers die elementaren Lebensäußerungen der handelnden Personen in besonderer Deutlichkeit hervortreten sollten? Die Indianer wurden von den weißen Amerikanern oft mit Herablassung und Geringschätzigkeit betrachtet. In dieser Kurzgeschichte jedoch werden sie in ihrer Menschlichkeit gezeigt, in ihrer Fähigkeit einander zu helfen, zu leiden, mitzuleiden; letztlich auch in ihrer Fähigkeit zu lieben. Die üblichen Klischees, die normalerweise mit Indianern verbunden sind, werden in dieser Geschichte hinterfragt; etwa der sprichwörtliche Stoizismus der Indianer: die Indianerin schreit andauernd, Nicks Vater hingegen ist der ruhige, überlegene Arzt, der unbeirrt seine Arbeit tut. Und der junge Indianer, der seinen eigenen, durch die Axtverletzung zugezogenen Schmerz geduldig ertragen hat, und der scheinbar stoisch unbewegt im oberen Etagenbett liegt, kann den Schmerz seiner jungen Frau nicht ertragen und nimmt sich das Leben. Was sagt dies wohl aus über des Indianers Liebe zu seiner Frau? Auch über diese Frage könnte diskutiert werden.

The Killers

Hemingways Short Story „The Killers" ist wegen ihres spannenden Inhalts, ihres dramatisch-szenenhaft angelegten Aufbaus, der anschaulichen, stark dialogischen Sprache, aber auch wegen ihres Gehalts (der provozierenden Aussage über die Beschaffenheit der Welt, in der Nick Adams zum Erwachsenen heranwächst) für die Durchnahme im Englischunterricht in besonderem Maße geeignet. Obschon sie durchaus in einem Grundkurs oder sogar in einem Leistungskurs behandelt werden könnte, eignet sich die Kurzgeschichte vor allem für eine 11. Klasse. Da die sprachlichen Schwierigkeiten gering sind, wäre es auch möglich, „The Killers" bereits in einer 10. Klasse zu lesen, wobei sich ein etwas zügigeres Vorgehen als in den Stundenblättern skizziert empfehlen würde.

Es ist allerdings davor zu warnen, diese Short Story nur *at its surface value* zu nehmen. Hemingways Sprache ist von einer trügerischen Einfachheit, und es ist nur zu leicht möglich, über manche Bezüge hinwegzulesen, Zeichen nicht zu erkennen und das, was ausgespart oder impliziert wird, nicht zu beachten. Da es sich bei den „Killers" zudem um eine besonders spannende Geschichte handelt, besteht um so mehr die Gefahr, daß die Schüler einfach darauflos lesen, um zu sehen, wie das Geschehen schließlich endet. Daher wird im folgenden vorgeschlagen, die Short Story in mehrere Abschnitte zu untergliedern und diese schrittweise zu behandeln.

Die Kurzgeschichte teilt sich bei genauerem Hinsehen in eine Reihe von insgesamt vier „Szenen". Die erste, dramatischste und zugleich längste ist die Lunchroom-Episode: zwei Gangster nisten sich im Lokal ein und treffen ihre Vorbereitungen zur Ermordung eines Schwergewichtsboxers, ziehen schließlich aber unverrichteter Dinge wieder ab, weil das Opfer nicht erscheint. Die zweite und äußerst wichtige Szene lenkt die Aufmerksamkeit auf den jungen Nick Adams, der zufällig Zeuge des Überfalls geworden ist, eine Stunde geknebelt und mit dem Koch zusammengefesselt in der Küche verbracht hat, und dann befreit wird. Von ihm wird nunmehr eine Entscheidung verlangt: soll er das riskante Unterfangen wagen, den Boxer aufzusuchen und ihn davor zu warnen, daß ihm die gedungenen Mörder auf den Fersen sind – oder lieber nicht?

In der dritten „Szene" sucht Nick den Schwergewichtsboxer in einem Hotel auf, um ihn zu retten, muß aber die frustrierende Erfahrung machen, daß der Boxer sich bereits aufgegeben hat und nur darauf wartet, erschossen zu werden.

Vierte und letzte „Szene": Wieder in den Lunchroom zurückgekehrt, versucht Nick vergeblich, das Erlebte zu verarbeiten und beschließt plötzlich, die Stadt zu verlassen. Er ist noch zu jung, um die Handlungsweisen, mit denen er in den letzten Stunden konfrontiert worden ist, begreifen zu können; er findet die Vorstellung unerträglich, daß da jemand in einem Hotelzimmer auf den Fangschuß wartet. Er leidet unter der grausamen Selbstverständlichkeit, mit der sich Brutalität und Gewissenlosigkeit, Zynismus, Gleichmut, Feigheit und Resignation behaupten, und verspürt den Wunsch, davonzulaufen.

So wie der kleine Nick in „Indian Camp" durch ein grausiges Erlebnis einen Blick in die Welt der Erwachsenen getan und eine neue Dimension kennengelernt hat, so lernt auch der heranwachsende Nick durch die unverhoffte Begegnung mit den Killern ei-

Übersicht über die Unterrichtseinheit „The Killers"

Stunde	Zentrales Stundenthema	Text	Stundeninhalt
1	I a) Customers in Henry's Lunch-room	from the beginning to: "I'll take ham and eggs," the man called Al said.	Background information. Leads up to the short story "The Killers". Discussion of the setting. / Exposition.
2	I b) Al's and Max's Strange Behaviour	from: He wore a derby hat... to: "What would we do to a nigger?"	Traces the development of a sense of danger. Growing tension.
3	I c) Preparation for Murder	from: George opened the slit... to: George looked up at the clock.	Detailed analysis and description of the scene. Movie clichés become reality: the face of ruthlessness.
4	I d) Waiting for the Kill	from: "If anybody comes in..." to: The two of them went out the door.	Introduces the elements of high level tension. The clock: "the time is out of joint."
5	II Nick's Conflict	from: George watched them... to: "I'll go up there."	Discussion of the importance of the boy's choice between involvement or evasion.
6	III Nick's Involvement	from: Outside the arc-light shone... to: "Good night," the woman said.	Anticlimax: A man up against the wall frustrates Nick's efforts.
7	IV Nick's Lesson	from: Nick walked up the dark street... to the end	Discussion of the result of Nick's experience. The short story, its structure and its meaning is reviewed. Nick's encounter with evil in this world. The pain of initiation.

nen neuen erschreckenden Lebensbereich kennen. Er wird noch einige Begegnungen und Erfahrungen dieser Art auf dem Weg ins Erwachsenwerden hinter sich bringen müssen. „The Killers" ist also eine *initiation story,* so wie „Indian Camp" und „The Battler" auch. Nick, nicht mehr Kind und noch nicht Erwachsener, muß lernen, was menschliche Existenz in dieser Welt meint.

Zum methodischen Vorgehen

Im Gegensatz zu anderen Hemingway-Kurzgeschichten (z. B. „Indian Camp", „Old Man at the Bridge" oder „Cat in the Rain") empfiehlt sich bei „The Killers" keine vorherige Gesamtlektüre der Geschichte, sondern das schrittweise Vorgehen, damit einerseits die Spannungssteigerung in der

Short Story leichter nachvollziehbar wird, zum anderen aber auch Schülerspekulationen über mögliche Entwicklungen miteingebracht werden können. Mit zunehmender Erfahrung im Umgang mit Kurzgeschichten werden die Schüler im „entdeckenden Lesen" geübt.

Grundsätzliche methodische Überlegungen, etwa zur Bedeutung einer kurzen Paraphrase vor der Textausdeutung, oder zum Tafelanschrieb, zur Ergebnissicherung, usw., werden im Einleitungsteil, S. 9 ff., dargestellt.

Es wäre gut, wenn für die Stunden 1 und 2, 3 und 4, 6 und 7 jeweils Doppelstunden zur Verfügung stünden; eine entsprechende Modifikation der Hausaufgabenstellung und gegebenenfalls der gelegentliche Einbau einer Stillphase müßten dann berücksichtigt werden.

Anmerkung: „The Killers" wurde zweimal verfilmt. 1946 schrieb Anthony Veiller ein Screenplay nach der Kurzgeschichte; die Verfilmung besorgte Robert Siodmak. Hauptdarsteller: Burt Lancaster und Ava Gardner. – 1964 Neuverfilmung durch Donald Siegel, Screenplay G. C. Loon; Darsteller: Lee Marvin, John Cassavetes, Angie Dickinson, Ronald Reagan. – Beide Filme sind freie Hollywood-Ausschmückungen des Handlungsgerüsts, für den Einsatz im Unterricht weder erhältlich noch geeignet.

Dennoch könnte der Lehrer gelegentlich diese Verfilmungen erwähnen; zum einen, da Hemingway ohnehin ganz bewußt gewisse Hollywood-Klischees aufgreift und akzentuiert, die er dann in erschreckende Realität umsetzt; zum anderen, weil die Szenenhaftigkeit dieser Kurzgeschichte geradezu „filmisch" angelegt ist; und schließlich auch, weil die Schüler es sicher reizvoll finden, sich bekannte Stars (wie Ronald Reagan!) in den Rollen vorzustellen.

1. Stunde:
A Seemingly Harmless Exposition

Unterrichtsschritt 1:
Hinführung zur Short Story „The Killers"

Schülern fällt die Bewältigung des Inhalts einer Kurzgeschichte leichter, wenn sie von vorneherein über ein gewisses Maß an Hintergrund- und Sachinformationen verfügen, die ihnen das Geschehen nachvollziehbar machen. Dies gilt vor allem für Hemingways Kriegsgeschichten, die einiger historischer Daten und Erläuterungen bedürfen; es gilt aber auch für die Nick-Adams-Geschichten, in denen die Landschaft des Mittelwestens Amerikas eine wesentliche Rolle spielt, da die „Helden" Hemingways – wenn auch unaufdringlich – in ständiger Wechselbeziehung zu ihrer Umgebung stehen. Darum empfiehlt es sich auch bei den „Killers", zunächst eine Hinführung zum „Raum" dieser Short Story zu versuchen, womit zugleich eine Einstimmung in die Atmosphäre zu Beginn der Geschichte angestrebt werden kann.

Man kann davon ausgehen, daß die Schüler über mehrere Jahre hinweg im Englischunterricht auf der Mittelstufe immer wieder mit der Thematik der „big city problems" konfrontiert worden sind. Sie haben daher eine gewisse Vorstellung von den Verhältnissen in amerikanischen Großstädten, vor allem natürlich von New York. Weniger vertraut sind sie hingegen mit dem „anderen Amerika", dem Amerika der kleinen und kleinsten *communities,* die meist pittoreske Namen vorweisen, auch wenn sie zuweilen nur aus einer Handvoll Häusern bestehen. Daher bietet es sich an, in einem Gespräch zunächst einmal über diesen Gegensatz zwischen den (wenigen) Großstädten und den unzähligen kleinen Nestern Amerikas zu sprechen, dabei die schier endlose Weite des Landes in Erinnerung zu rufen, das von einem Netz schnurgerader Landstraßen durchzogen wird, auf denen *truckers* (= *truck drivers*) ihre schweren Lastwagen steuern ...

Vielleicht sollte der Lehrer die Klasse zu einem Gedankenexperiment auffordern. "Let's get on one of those trucks, shall we? Let's join a trucker on his westbound route from Chicago to San Francisco, California. What would such a journey be like?" Zur Sprache kämen dann einige für die Situation charakteristische Umstände wie: *monotonous driving, the endless stretch of the highways, the commercials on the radio interrupted by CB radio jokes from other truckers ...*

Der Lehrer könnte dann bewußt steuernd selbst einen Beitrag leisten, indem er den Verlauf der Fahrt weiter beschreibt, etwa: "Hilly landscape at first, then the Plains. The land as flat as a board. Then a slight incline, just a little hill, not much to speak of. A couple of houses. What did the sign say? 'Summit' – well, the inhabitants must have a sense of humour! Anyway, they've got a gas station here, and a roadside lunch-counter. May as well stop here and get a bite to eat. Doesn't look too bad, that place. Let's take a look at their menu. Hm, the same as usual, ham and eggs, hamburgers, cheeseburgers ... can't they think of anything else? Ah, that doesn't sound bad, though: liver and bacon ... Well then, in we go!"

Auf diese Weise wird ein doppeltes Ziel erreicht. Zum einen wird die Umgebung eines unbedeutenden und auch geographisch nicht genauer fixierten kleinen Ortes charakterisiert (und auch die Ironie der Ortsbezeichnung „Summit" bewußt mitaufgegriffen); es wird deutlich, was ein Lunchroom ist, und zum anderen wird in diesem Hinführungsgespräch bereits Vokabular eingeführt, das zum Verständnis des Beginns der Kurzgeschichte benötigt wird.

Der Einsatz geeigneter Dias (*small towns in the USA / road-side taverns / gas station*) wäre denkbar, ist aber nicht unbedingt notwendig. (Hinweis: In seinem Buch „Hemingway's Nick Adams" versucht J. M. Flora nachzuweisen, wo in Michigan und Illinois sich Nick Adams bewegt, und lokalisiert auch Summit als einen konkreten Ort in der Nähe von Chicago. Vgl. Literaturverzeichnis.)

Wenn wie oben vorgeschlagen verfahren wird, können die zum Verständnis notwendigen Vokabeln (*lunch-room, counter, menu, pork tenderloin, liver and bacon*) im Unterrichtsgespräch geklärt werden. Sie sollten auf der (zugeklappten) Tafel notiert werden und zunächst – während des Lehrervortrags – sichtbar sein.

Unterrichtsschritt 2:
Textpräsentation

Aus mehreren Gründen empfiehlt es sich, daß der Lehrer selbst den Anfang der den Schülern noch unbekannten Short Story vorträgt. Durch das Hinführungsgespräch sind die Schüler auf den Inhalt der Geschichte gespannt. Der Lehrer kann durch sein „interpretierendes Lesen" des Anfangs die Spannungs- und Erwartungshaltung weiter verstärken. Zugleich kann er das Hörverständnis seiner Schüler überprüfen. Ein Einschnitt bietet sich an nach "I'll take ham and eggs, the man called Al said", da bis zu dieser Stelle die Situation im Lunchroom noch relativ normal ist und die *two men* noch nicht näher beschrieben werden.

Die Texte der Schüler werden erst nach dem Lehrervortrag aufgeschlagen. Eine kurze Stillesephase kann sich anschließen, in der die Schüler den Anfang der Short Story noch einmal für sich durchlesen, gegebenenfalls mit Rückfragen nach eventuell noch unbekannten Wörtern. Vor dem Gespräch über den Anfang der Geschichte sollte der Abschnitt noch einmal von einem guten Schüler vorgelesen werden.

Zur Überprüfung des Globalverständnisses wird eine knappe Paraphrase verlangt, zunächst ohne auf Details einzugehen. Sollten die Schüler jedoch bereits präzise Beobachtungen mitteilen, könnten diese für den Tafelanschrieb verwertet werden.

Unterrichtsschritt 3:
Besprechung der „setting" und der erwähnten Personen

The students are asked to state where the story opens, at what time of day and in what season; how many characters there are in the room, and what we learn about them. The findings are noted down in the board diagram.

If the students do not notice the abrupt beginning of the story ("The door ... opened and two men came in.") although it could remind them of typical scenes in Western movies where swinging saloon doors are usually part of the scene, and if they don't pay a great deal of attention to the title of the story at first, this should not concern the teacher too much; it could prove rather an advantage for the subsequent step-by-step analysis.

To begin with, Hemingway seems to describe a very common everyday situation: two men enter a restaurant, Henry's lunchroom, and want something to eat. They have not made up their minds yet as to what they would like to eat, and unenthusiastically study the menu. But then one of them decides, and is a bit annoyed when George, the barkeeper and waiter, tells them that they can't get dinner before six o'clock and that they'll have to content themselves with something simple, such as ham and eggs.

Besides the waiter there is only one other person in the room, Nick Adams, who is sitting at some distance from the men, at the end of the counter, watching them. Nick is the only person whose full name is mentioned; the waiter is referred to by his first name only, and up to this point only the first name of one of the men (Al) has been

revealed in their conversation. Nick seems to know George well, they "had been talking".

Outside, the street-lights have come on. Considering it is only five o'clock the time of the year must ·be either late fall or winter. (Later on in the story the bare branches of trees are mentioned and towards the end of the story Mrs Bell speaks of a "nice fall day like this"; so the season is late fall.)

Summing up what little information we can draw from the opening of the short story we can say that we are concerned with "an ordinary everyday situation". (→ T 1) This conclusion leads to a brief look at the language of this introductory passage.

Unterrichtsschritt 4:
Besprechung der Sprachebene

Hier genügen zunächst einige wenige Kommentare. Da gerade von einer normalen Alltagssituation in einem Lokal die Rede ist, bereitet es den Schülern keine Schwierigkeit, auch die Sprache der Short Story als Alltagssprache zu charakterisieren, zumal sie hier überwiegend aus Dialogen besteht. Auch dieser Sachverhalt wird an der Tafel festgehalten, ohne daß an dieser Stelle etwa schon auf die Hintergründigkeit und die *deceiving simplicity* des Hemingwayschen Stils eingegangen wird.

Hausaufgabe:

Mit der Einstimmung in die Atmosphäre dieser Geschichte ist nunmehr die Voraussetzung für die folgende Entwicklung des Außergewöhnlichen aus dem Gewöhnlichen heraus gewonnen. Wenn die Schüler den Anfang der Geschichte zu Hause noch einmal lesen und dann weiterlesen bis "... What would we do to a nigger?", wird ihnen deutlich werden, wie sich aus der scheinbar *ordinary situation* des Anfangs eine *extraordinary situation* entwickelt, in der eine im-

34

mer stärker gespannte Atmosphäre entsteht. Die Schüler sollen die unbekannten Vokabeln (möglichst in einem einsprachigen Wörterbuch) nachschlagen und auf einem separaten Bogen notieren. Ein eigenes Kollokationsfeld anzulegen, bietet sich hier nicht an, also genügt der thematische Zusammenhang. (Der Lehrer sollte gelegentlich deutlich machen, welche Wörter nicht aktiv gelernt zu werden brauchen.)

2. Stunde:
Development of a Sense of Danger/ Growing Tension

Unterrichtsschritt 1:
Wiederholung der Ergebnisse

Es ist wichtig, daß zu Beginn der Stunde der Text der Kurzgeschichte, soweit er bis jetzt vorbereitet wurde, noch einmal von Anfang an vorgelesen wird. Ein Schüler liest bis ". . . the man called Al said.", ein zweiter liest weiter bis "What would we do to a nigger?" Erfahrungsgemäß verlockt der überwiegend aus Dialog bestehende Text dieser Short Story mit seinen kurzen Sätzen die Schüler sehr rasch zu guter, die Situation angemessen interpretierender Intonation. Gelegentliches Eingreifen des Lehrers mag notwendig werden, um eine Satzintonation zu verbessern oder um einen besonderen Akzent zu setzen.
Im Anschluß an den Lesevortrag erfolgt eine kurze Rekapitulation der *setting, persons* und *atmosphere* zu Beginn der Kurzgeschichte.
Es empfiehlt sich, das in der 1. Stunde erarbeitete Tafelbild auf Folie zu schreiben; diese kann nach der kurzen Wiederholung aufgelegt und sodann um den in der Stunde fälligen Anschrieb ergänzt werden. Durch Pfeile werden Bezüge im Tafelanschrieb verdeutlicht.

Unterrichtsschritt 2:
Al's and Max's Strange Behaviour

As a matter of principle a brief paraphrase of the passage to be discussed should precede the actual text analysis, even if the students claim that they have understood everything. At this point in "The Killers" it might be useful to note some striking points about the two men who have entered the lunch-room.
First of all their unusual apparel should be noted: derby hat, black overcoat, silk scarf, gloves – this description might prompt the students to remember stereotypes in old Hollywood gangster films (Humphrey Bogart may come to mind.). Next, Al's face is described (small, white, tight-lipped), its whiteness accentuating a stark contrast with the black derby hat and the black overcoat. We wonder why his face is so white; has Al perhaps shunned the light of the sun? Has he reason to avoid the open daylight? We remember that the men appear at a time when it is getting dark outside; and the street-lights are coming on.
What else can we say about the two men? They have different faces, but they are "dressed like twins". Both of them wear tightly buttoned overcoats, both of them keep their derby hats on, and also their gloves. (This in itself characterizes them as 'birds of a feather'.) Keeping their hats on may just be bad manners, or sheer negligence, but why don't they take their gloves off if they intend to eat food? Are they afraid of leaving fingerprints? Tight overcoats, tight lips – the meagre description of the two men, given late and in outlines only, suddenly makes them appear sinister. Their names, too, are somewhat unusual; the name 'Al' might remind some students of Al Capone, the famous Italo-American gang-

ster boss of the Twenties; the other man's name, Max, which is revealed relatively late in the dialogue, indicates German origin.

How do Al and Max behave after they have ordered their food? The students' attention should be drawn to the gradual change in tone and behaviour of the two men; they should be alerted to Hemingway's revealing handling of the dialogue in the following passage. (The answer to the question accompanying their homework should be incorporated in the ensuing observations.) The men ask for something "to drink", and George tells them what soft drinks he has to offer, at which Al reacts with exaggerated irony, making it obvious that he was thinking of alcoholic drinks, although he must be aware of the prohibition laws of the time. (Note: Prohibition in the USA was enacted from 1917 until 1933.) No doubt George is used to rather rough language in his lunchroom, where he caters for down-to-earth men such as farm hands and truck drivers, but in the questions and comments of these two smartly dressed customers there are ironical undertones which become increasingly provocative, and eventually insolent and insulting.

How do George and Nick react to the men's unexpectedly insulting behaviour? George remains quite cool, disregards the irony, does not fall for any provocation. When Max, with a great deal of sarcasm, comments on "the big dinner" George even responds willingly with "That's right." This response, however, prompts Max to take George literally. "So you think that's right?" The ironically superficial exchange of questions and remarks is suddenly charged with dangerous undertones. The sense of danger is intensified when Al, provocatively, calls George "bright boy" and, adding insult to injury, when before turning to Nick, he makes his final whip-lash comment "He's dumb". George prudently swallows the of-

fence without showing any reaction. Again, when he serves the men and makes sure he gets their order right he accepts Max's biting "bright boy" without a word. (Note that in the end Max takes the ham and eggs Al had ordered; obviously, the two men are not in the least interested in the type of food they are about to eat.) And when Max attacks George just for having looked at him – a drastic increase in tension – George tries to relieve the unbearably tense situation by complying with Al's words ("Maybe the boy (!) meant it for a joke.") and laughing, but again he is brutally rebuked, is forbidden to laugh, and is subjected to further ironical and offensive remarks. Only once does he put up a feeble defence with his "Where do you think you are?", but this attempt to stand up to the bullies is no more than rhetorical and is repulsed by Max's threatening reply.

So far Nick has just been a quiet witness of the scene. When asked by Al, what his name was, Nick, strangely enough, only says "Adams", his last name. This unwillingness to yield any more information than is necessary may be taken as a sign of his resentment, a subconscious refusal on the part of the boy, who doesn't know what to make of the situation but senses its immanent danger. Al doesn't take any notice of Nick's name anyhow; a little later he asks again what his name is, but without waiting for an answer, when he harshly sends Nick to join George behind the counter.

Nick doesn't understand what is going on, but of course he registers the ironical insolence of the continually repeated "bright boy" and the frivolous implication of "your boyfriend". His question "What's the idea?" shows his confusion and irritation; also, he is bound to realize the thinly veiled threat in Al's response "You better go around, bright boy." Nick does as he is told.

Then George takes up Nick's question and asks, twice, with increasing intensity,

"What's the idea?" thus conveying to the reader a greatly heightened sense of danger. But the two men are in no mood for an explanation. Al cuts any discussion short with a furious "What the hell do you argue with this kid (!) for?" and with an imperative and threatening "Listen, tell the nigger to come out here." he puts an end to the discussion. The give-and-take ends with George's portentous question "What are you going to do to him?" and a sarcastic answer with horrible implications, "Nothing. Use your head, bright boy. What would we do to a nigger?"; then George obeys and calls the cook.

Looking back over the introductory part of the short story the students could be asked to sum up in a few sentences the development of a situation that initially seemed no more than an ordinary everyday encounter in a lunch-room, into an increasingly tense, offensive and implicitly dangerous atmosphere that culminates in Al's nonchalant sarcasm with regard to the "nigger", revealing as it does, Al's mercilessly unscrupulous attitude.

Unterrichtsschritt 3: (fakultativ)
Analyse der Sprache

Wenn es die Zeit erlaubt, sollte in einem Exkurs die Aufmerksamkeit der Schüler darauf gelenkt werden, mit welchen sprachlichen Mitteln Hemingway seine Wirkung erzielt. Hemingway hat für diese Short Story überwiegend die Dialogform gewählt, wodurch die Dramatik des Geschehens unterstrichen wird. "The Killers" liest sich fast wie ein Filmskript; nur ganz wenige, kurze beschreibende Passagen sind eingeflochten. Die Sprache des Dialogs, vor allem die immer schärfer hervortretende Aggressivität in den Äußerungen der beiden Gangster, bestimmt die Atmosphäre. Die zum Schluß des besprochenen Abschnitts verwendeten Imperative "You go around on the other side...", "Tell him to come in...", "Tell him...", "tell the nigger to..." unterstreichen die Schärfe des Tons.

Unterrichtsschritt 4:
Dialogische Präsentation des Textes

Nachdem die Schüler den Anteil des Sprachlichen an der Wirkung des Textes auf den Leser reflektiert haben, soll der Anfang der Short Story bis "What would we do to a nigger?" abschließend noch einmal gelesen werden, und zwar mit verteilten Rollen. In einer kurzen Stillphase kennzeichnen die Schüler die jeweiligen Sprecher vor den Zeilen. Dann tragen vier Schüler den Text möglichst realistisch vor (der Lehrer kann die verbindenden Passagen lesen), wobei sie sich darum bemühen sollten, die zunehmende Bedrohlichkeit der Situation deutlich werden zu lassen.

Hausaufgabe:

Neben der Vorbereitung des folgenden Textabschnitts (bis "George looked up at the clock.") mit einer begleitenden Leitfrage sollen sich die Schüler die reale Situation im Lunchroom verdeutlichen, indem sie versuchen, eine Skizze des Lokals anzufertigen (*counter, mirror, clock, door, wicket, position of George and Max on the two sides of the counter, and Al behind the wicket*).

3. Stunde:
Preparation for Murder

Unterrichtsschritt 1:
Überprüfen der Hausaufgabe

Die Kontrolle der Kenntnis einiger Wörter (wie z. B. *stool, wicket, kosher*) dient dazu, den Schülern gelegentlich zu zeigen, daß die häusliche Vorbereitung des Textes auch auf diese Weise überprüft wird. Außerdem wird wahrscheinlich das Verständnis der Anzüglichkeit "You were in a kosher convent. That's where you were." bei der späteren Besprechung erleichtert.

Unterrichtsschritt 2:
Lesen des häuslich vorbereiteten Textes

Ein guter Schüler trägt den Textabschnitt von "George opened the slit..." bis "George looked up at the clock." vor.

Unterrichtsschritt 3:
Further Steps in the Development of the Situation

Starting from the question that accompanied the students' homework, "What are the further steps in the development of the situation in the lunch-room?" the continuing course of the action is traced. When Sam, the cook, a black man, is called in, Al addresses him contemptuously as "nigger"and tells him harshly to stay where he is. Sam takes one look at the two men at the counter and immediately recognizes their dangerousness. Willingly he tolerates being bossed around and responds to Al's command with an obedient "Yes, sir." (!) He voices neither surprise nor protest, and completely submits to the situation. He is taken back into the kitchen by Al, and Nick is ordered to join them. Nick, too, obeys without any comment. We learn only afterwards what Al does with Nick and the cook in the kitchen.

Meanwhile Max keeps looking past George at the mirror on the wall behind the counter. Three times his looking at the mirror is mentioned. It will be clear to the students that he has an eye on the entrance door of the lunch-room in the mirror, although we don't know the reason for this yet. Tension grows.

At this point the students might be asked to draw a sketch on the board of the layout of the lunch-counter situation indicating the position of counter, saloon-mirror, entrance, door to kitchen with wicket, etc. (→ T 3 und Illustration)

George's faint "What's it all about?" provokes derisive comments both from Max and from Al in the kitchen. When Al suggests to Max "Why don't you tell him?" we sense that under these circumstances whatever they have come for must be something of terrible importance; and when George – asked to venture his own suggestion – recoils with "I wouldn't say", the implication again is that the thoughts in his mind are too horrible to be uttered. We are alerted further when we realize that these last sentences were only spoken to test whether Al in the kitchen could understand well enough what is being said in the lunch-room. Through the wicket in the door leading to the kitchen Al then gives his orders, short, determined, imperative, "like a photographer arranging for a group picture." "Listen, bright boy... Stand a little farther...", "You move..." He groups his pal Max and George like a producer giving stage directions. Why does he arrange their positions in such a manner? While a terrible suspicion is beginning to grow in the reader, Max, without being asked at this moment, unexpectedly yields the stupendous information, "We're going to kill a Swede."

The enormity of these words, spoken with cold, casual assertiveness, is balanced by

George's seemingly indifferent reaction. George behaves as if nothing particular or extraordinary was happening. In fact, however, it is obvious that at this moment the brutal face of ruthlessness is showing without any disguise. The two men are determined killers who have set a trap for Ole Andreson, a Swede; Al is probably going to shoot him through the wicket. As before, George tries to keep cool, not to be provoked by the gangsters, and in turn, not to provoke them. So he answers their questions about Ole Andreson's habit of coming to the lunch-room with strategic precision.

When Max suddenly asks George, "Ever go to the movies?" he seems, for a moment, to change the subject; but, in fact he doesn't. Innumerable times Hollywood gangster films have shown such cliché situations as hold-ups and killings in great realistic detail, and are familiar fare to the average movie-goer. However, these films are of course consumed from the safe distance of a movie theatre armchair and thus take place in a fictitious and removed "reality". But in Henry's lunch-room the movie setting has suddenly turned into an immediate and most pressing reality. Those two men don't just look like "baddies", they are, in fact, gangsters. Hired killers who are prepared to shoot a Swede "for a friend. Just to oblige a friend..." They don't even know their victim, Ole Andreson. "He never seen us." Al's cynical comment, "And he's only going to see us once." (namely at the moment when Ole is killed) reveals him as an entirely pitiless, hard-core, ice-cold criminal. He seems to be the more intelligent of the two gangsters, and although both he and Max speak rather sloppily, Max's use of language is somewhat more primitive and faulty than Al's. Al is the tougher of the two: he arranges the scene for the killing, he is probably the one who will shoot, and he states that Max is talking too much, thus indicating

that those present, namely George, Sam and Nick, receive too much information which they might use as witnesses against the gangsters.

His "joke" "I got them tied up like a couple of girlfriends in the convent" now informs us about what has happened to Sam and Nick in the kitchen. Al does not run any risk of being disturbed in his job! The reader drawing on his movie experience can picture the situation in the kitchen and can supply the rest of the information himself: if the two are tied together they are presumably gagged as well.

(The frivolous ambiguity of "girlfriends in the convent" need not be discussed; nor is the ironical juxtaposition of "kosher" and "convent", i.e. of Jewish and Catholic religious terms, particularly funny; it seems to suggest, though, that Max is Jewish.)

George, now in complete possession of the facts, looks up at the clock, thus revealing his nervousness and inner tension. Ole should be appearing soon. The stage is set for murder.

Hausaufgabe:

Das Herausarbeiten des genauen Zeitablaufs (falsche Zeitanzeige/wirkliche Zeit) mit stichwortartigem Festhalten des jeweiligen Geschehens wird die Besprechung in der 4. Stunde erleichtern.

4. Stunde:
Waiting for the Kill

Unterrichtsschritt 1:
Lesen des vorbereiteten Abschnitts

Der Text wird von "If anybody comes in . . ." bis "The two of them went out the door." gelesen. Durch die durchgängig dialogische Form dieser Kurzgeschichte sind die Schüler inzwischen an einen guten, interpretierenden Lesevortrag gewöhnt. Sie werden dazu angehalten, sich in die Rolle des jeweils Sprechenden hineinzuversetzen, um eine möglichst echte Intonation zu erreichen.

Unterrichtsschritt 2:
Waiting for the Kill

In a short paraphrase of the passage the students state that the expected victim, Ole Andreson, does not appear at 6 o'clock; however, the gangsters continue waiting while other customers enter and leave the lunch-room. Eventually, at 7 o'clock, Al and Max give up and leave the place.

The students' attention is drawn to the clock and the times mentioned; their homework (a time schedule of the sequence of events) should be referred to. Starting point for a class discussion could be the question at what time the killers actually expect Ole Andreson. The board diagram (→ T 4) should clarify the confusion caused by the lunch-room clock being twenty minutes fast. We remember that when the two men order a meal in Henry's lunch-room at 5 o'clock, the clock on the wall behind the counter shows twenty past five, much to their irritation. The clock anticipates a point in time which has actually not arrived yet. This is, of course, an additional element of suspense: when the clock has already passed Ole's expected time of arrival, the real target time

is still imminent. This also explains why George keeps looking up at the clock when Max briefs him how to respond to chance customers.

Max's instructions are given in a commanding, bossy manner, allowing for no discussion or comment. George, as before, complies without contradiction; what is really going on inside him is expressed only indirectly: his question "What are you going to do with us afterwards?" reveals that he is already thinking of the moment after Ole's assassination and of the consequences for himself. (This constitutes another time shift: George's thoughts run, like the clock, ahead of the time and anticipate events that have not taken place yet.) As one who can assess the situation realistically he is well aware of the fact that he himself, and also the cook and Nick, run the risk of being shot dead as witnesses of the crime, when everything is over. Max's answer, "That'll depend. That's one of the things you never know at the time." can only serve to confirm his anticipation, as obviously it contains a terrible threat.

The students should realize the implications of such questions and answers. Also, they should notice how tension is increased by Hemingway's use of dramatic effects. "It was a quarter past six. The door from the street opened." A quarter past six means it is in fact only five to six; is Ole arriving a couple of minutes early perhaps? "The door . . . opened." – a moment of great tension. Then we find that instead of Ole some other customer enters, a streetcar motorman, and our tension is relaxed again. (The students may notice the theatricality of the line and will remember similar scenes from spine-chilling movies such as Hitchcock's: at the moment of highest tension a door opens slowly and – comic relief – a cat sneaks in.)

After George has managed to get rid of the motorman he looks up at the clock again. It says twenty past six now, which is, in fact, six o'clock, – the target time. The face of the clock, which mistakenly shows a time that has not arrived yet, becomes a constant point of reference for the characters in the story as well as for the reader.

By writing the correct times step by step next to the falsely shown times of the clock (in a board diagram) as they are mentioned in the text, the skilful technique with which Hemingway manages on the one hand to further heighten the reader's tension, and on the other hand to symbolize the growing insecurity brought about by the cruel destruction of order can be demonstrated. Thus the clock epitomises the fact that (in Hamlet's words) "the time is out of joint."

George acts exactly as he has been told to. He obliges. "A regular little gentleman", as Max comments sarcastically. However, the next line reveals that George has no other choice: Al's gun is pointed at him! "He knew I'd blow his head off," Al says from the kitchen.

The way Al is described now clearly reveals him as a professional killer, almost the classical stereotype of a gangster: "derby hat tipped back", "the muzzle of a sawed-off (!) shotgun resting on the ledge". He has tied up Nick and Sam in the back of the room, and has gagged their mouths with towels. We can assume now that most likely Al was holding his gun in his hand while ordering the others about and arranging them so as to have a clear field of vision and unobstructed shooting range; but Hemingway doesn't mention when the gun is first displayed. Perhaps we can also draw some conclusions now as to the way the gangsters are dressed: their tight-fitting overcoats buttoned across the chest would not interfere with fast movements in an emergency, whereas the wider lower parts allow for their guns to be pocketed inconspicuously, leaving just "a slight bulge".

Several times George tries to convince the gangsters that it is no use waiting any longer. At 6.55 (i. e. 6.35!) he says, "He's not coming", and again, "Your friend (!) . . . isn't going to come." But this cuts no ice with the gangsters. Unmoved, almost casual, Max "gives" Ole another ten minutes. The retardation game continues; a seemingly relaxed outward appearance covering up extreme nervous strain. Max's eyes move from the mirror to the clock: the clock says 7.00 (i. e. 6.40), then 7.05 (i. e. 6.45). At last Max gives up. "We better go. He's not coming." But Al's patience is not exhausted yet. "Better give him five minutes." Another delay! When eventually Al, too, concedes that there is no use waiting for the Swede any longer, the situation suddenly comes to a point of extreme tension once more as Al asks a question with dreadful implications: "What about the two bright boys and the nigger?" He might have added: "Should we play it safe and shoot them so that they can't testify against us, or can we risk leaving them as they are?" Max believes: "They're all right", probably because George has proved that he is prepared to play along with them; Sam, the cook, is scared to death and will keep away from trouble; and Nick is obviously just "a kid", too young to be taken seriously. But Al remembers that Max has been talking too much and leaves the question open for another dangerous moment. When he, too, has made up his mind to leave without any bloodshed, his final words "You got a lot of luck", wholeheartedly supported by Max, indicate clearly that George, Sam and Nick have escaped death just by the skin of their teeth!

The line "The two of them went out the door." rounds off the first great "scene" of this short story, which begins with the door opening and the two men entering. The curve of tension drops now; the reader can relax.

Unterrichtsschritt 3:
Graphische Darstellung der Spannungskurve

Mit wenigen Strichen, ohne viel Zeitverlust, zeichnet ein Schüler die fieberkurvenartig ansteigende Spannungskurve an, die plötzlich abreißt, als die Gangster den Raum verlassen. Der nur kurz verdeutlichte Spannungsverlauf soll noch einmal optisch veranschaulichen, wie dieser erste Teil der Kurzgeschichte angelegt ist. Zugleich aber ist damit eine gewisse Vorarbeit intendiert für eine am Ende der Besprechung geplante graphische Darstellung der Gesamtentwicklung der Short Story (vgl. Stundenblatt).

Hausaufgabe:

Die Schüler werden sich wundern, nur eine relativ kurze Passage zur Vorbereitung zu bekommen. Wegen der Wichtigkeit dieser Stelle sollte man aber noch nicht weiter lesen lassen. Der zweite Teil der Hausaufgabe veranlaßt die Schüler nicht nur zu einem wiederholenden Rückblick über das bisher Gelesene, sondern auch zu einer Strukturierungsübung. Sie sollen Überschriften zu den (etwa fünf) feststellbaren Entwicklungsschritten finden.

5. Stunde:
Nick's Conflict

Unterrichtsschritt 1:
Rückblick über den Aufbau der Geschichte

Anknüpfend an die vorangegangene Stunde fassen die Schüler anhand ihrer Hausaufgabe das bisherige Geschehen mit einigen Sätzen zusammen. (Dabei charakterisieren sie vornehmlich Georges Verhalten.)

1. The story begins with a seemingly harmless exposition: two men enter a restaurant and order something to eat.

2. When they cannot get the dinner they want, they start bullying the waiter and Nick Adams, another guest.
3. Their tone and behaviour becomes more and more insulting and aggressive; but the waiter remains cool and keeps his head.
4. Eventually the men reveal themselves as gangsters preparing for the coldblooded murder of a guest (a boxer) expected to arrive at 6 o'clock.
5. For one hour the atmosphere in the lunch-room is charged with great tension as they wait for the boxer, who, however, does not come.
6. Tension is relieved when eventually the two gangsters leave without having accomplished their task.

Die Zusammenfassung dient als Überleitung zur folgenden Textstelle, in der Nick ins Zentrum des Interesses rückt.

Unterrichtsschritt 2:
Textpräsentation

Dieser Textteil (von "George watched them through the window..." bis "I'll go up there.") kann als die eigentliche „Mitte" der Kurzgeschichte bezeichnet werden. Zur besonderen Gewichtung empfiehlt sich hier ein Lehrervortrag; durch rollenadäquates Lesen, begleitet von entsprechender Mimik, auch gelegentlich ein leichtes Zögern beim Sprechen, sollte der Entscheidungskonflikt, in dem Nick steht, verdeutlicht werden.

Unterrichtsschritt 3:
Nick's Conflict

As part of their homework the students have to answer the question "How do George, Nick and the cook behave when the danger is over?" The students' observations, supported by the teacher's interpretative reading of the passage should make it clear that

T5

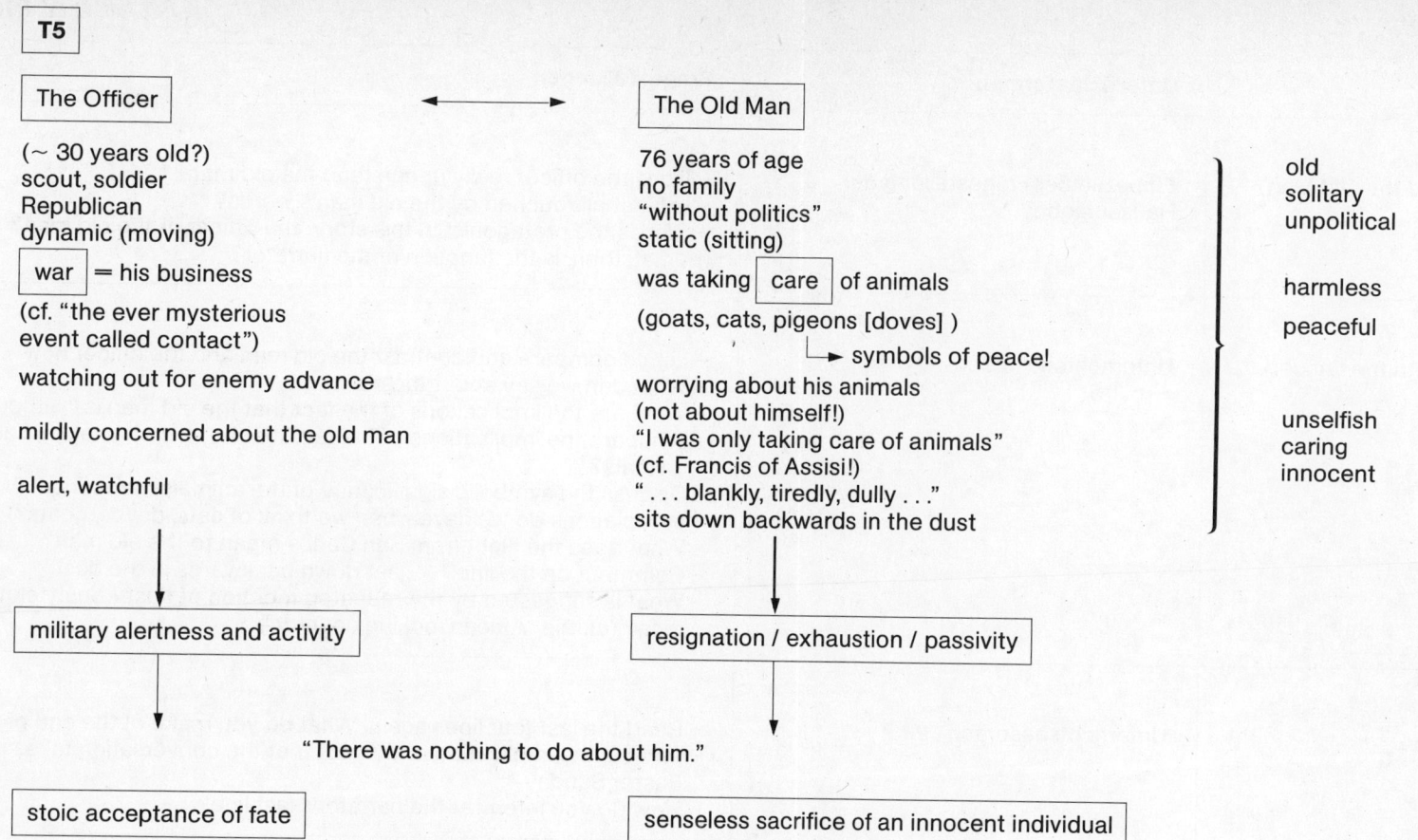

The Officer ←——→ **The Old Man**

The Officer	The Old Man	
(~ 30 years old?) scout, soldier Republican dynamic (moving)	76 years of age no family "without politics" static (sitting)	old solitary unpolitical
war = his business	was taking care of animals (goats, cats, pigeons [doves]) └→ symbols of peace!	harmless peaceful
(cf. "the ever mysterious event called contact")		
watching out for enemy advance	worrying about his animals (not about himself!) "I was only taking care of animals" (cf. Francis of Assisi!) " . . . blankly, tiredly, dully . . ." sits down backwards in the dust	unselfish caring innocent
mildly concerned about the old man		
alert, watchful		

military alertness and activity

resignation / exhaustion / passivity

"There was nothing to do about him."

stoic acceptance of fate

senseless sacrifice of an innocent individual

Unterrichtsschritte	Unterrichtsformen	Fragestellungen
1. Unterrichtsschritt: Does the Officer Understand the Old Man? Anknüpfen an vorige Stunde	Einbezug der Fragestellung der Hausaufgabe	– Does the officer really understand the old man? – Is he at all touched by the old man's words? – Who is the protagonist in this story: the officer or the old man? – What, then, is the function of the narrator?
2. Unterrichtsschritt: The Old Man Contrasted With the Officer	Unterrichtsgespräch ⟶ T 5	– Let us compare and contrast the old man and the officer now. – What can we say about the old man? – What are the implications of the fact that the old man is "without politics"? – What are the implications of the fact that he was only taking care of animals? – Discuss the symbolic significance of the animals mentioned. (What associations do we have when we think of cats, doves, goats?) – What does the flight from San Carlos mean to the old man? – Comment on the line " . . . sat down backwards in the dust." – What is suggested by the repeated mention of dust / dusty clothes / dusty face? (cf. the "African looking country")
3. Unterrichtsschritt: The Meaning of the End	Unterrichtsgespräch	– Read the last four lines again. What do you make of the end of the story? – What is the implication of the fact that the conversation takes place on Easter Sunday? – How do you interpret the narrator's last line?
4. Unterrichtsschritt: Abschließendes Lesen	Schüler-Lesevortrag	
5. Unterrichtsschritt: Weiterführende Fragestellungen		– If you have developed an interest in the way Hemingway portrays people involved in the Spanish Civil War you might want to read his novel "For Whom the Bell Tolls". – Try to imagine what it must be like to leave your home in a war situation. – Do you know any refugees? Where did they come from? Why did they flee? (Vietnam? Poland? Other Countries?)

1. Stunde: Getting to the Indian Camp

Unterrichtsschritte	Unterrichtsformen	Fragestellungen
Unterrichtsschritt 1: Hinführung zur Short Story „Indian Camp" a) Bereitstellen landeskundlicher Information	Unterrichtsgespräch Lehrerhinweise	– Where do North American Indians live nowadays? – Why do most of them live on reservations? – What is the difference between a reservation and a camp? – What kind of work do Indians do for the whites? For what reason? – What kind of job is bark-peeling? – Can you imagine what happens if an Indian worker gets ill?
b) Überprüfen einiger wichtiger Vokabeln	Vokabelkontrolle im situativen Zusammenhang	– Explain the meaning of: labour pain / Caesarian / an anaesthetic / incision / exhilaration
Unterrichtsschritt 2: Knappe Inhaltsangabe der ganzen Kurzgeschichte	Schülervortrag	– Give a brief summary of Hemingway's short story "Indian Camp"; leave out the details.
Unterrichtsschritt 3: Gliederung der Kurzgeschichte (Einbezug der Hausaufgabe)	Unterrichtsgespräch ⟶ T 1	– Into how many main parts could we divide this story? – Do you see possible further subdivisions? – What headings could we find for the five parts?
Unterrichtsschritt 4: The Exposition a) Lesen (Anfang – " . . . 'Oh', said Nick.")	Schüler-Lesevortrag	
b) Setting and the persons mentioned	Unterrichtsgespräch ⟶ T 2	– Where does the story open? – Who are the persons mentioned? / How are they described? – What actual information do we get about them? – Can you make any comment on Nick's father at this point? – Are there any words that seem to be of particular importance? If so, which? And why? – What can you say about the atmosphere at the beginning of the story? – What effect does the uncanny atmosphere of nightly cold and mist have on the reader?
c) Lesen ("Across the bay . . ." – " . . . holding a lamp.")	Schüler-Lesevortrag	
d) Getting to the camp	Unterrichtsgespräch ⟶ T 3	– What is described in this passage? – How is the men's journey described? – How would you characterize the atmosphere in the camp when the men arrive? – What do you call the opening of a story, with the description of the setting and the characters? – Comment on Hemingway's style in the exposition.

Homework:

Read the short story again.
Concentrate your attention on the main characters present before and during the Caesarian operation.
1. What can we say about Nick before and during the operation?
2. What about the young Indian father?
3. And what about Nick's father?

T1

| I   Getting to the Indian Camp |

| II a) Preparing the Operation
    b) The Operation .
    c) The Discovery of the Young Indian Father's Suicide |

| III Returning from the Indian Camp |

T3

| Getting to the Indian Camp: |

– crossing a dark and misty bay
– walking through a wet meadow into wood ⟶ trail ⟶ road ⟶ hills
– arrival at the Indian Camp (bark-peelers' shanties)

} brief, realistic matter-of-fact description

T2

SETTING:

a lake shore / a bay
2 rowing boats
night
darkness
mist on the water
cold

} atmosphere! }

PERSONS:

Nick
Nick's father (a doctor)
Uncle George

} rowed by two Indians to a "very sick Indian lady"

(Nick with his father's arm around him!)

Unterrichtsschritte	Unterrichtsformen	Fragestellungen
Unterrichtsschritt 1: Wiederholen der Ergebnisse a) Rekapitulation der „setting", „persons", „atmosphere" b) Die Funktion der Exposition	Kurzes Referieren durch mehrere Schüler Unterrichtsgespräch	– Let's recapitulate briefly what we said about the opening of Hemingway's short story "Indian Camp". – What effect is achieved by the opening passages of the story? – What then can we say about the function of the exposition?
Unterrichtsschritt 2: Preparing for the Operation a) Lesen ("Inside on a wooden bunk . . ." – ". . . 'I'd rather not touch it!'") b) Überprüfen des Textverständnisses Paraphrase des Textabschnitts mit gleichzeitiger Ausdeutung (Einbezug der Hausaufgabe)	Schüler-Lesevortrag Lehrer-Schüler-Gespräch (eventuell Skizze eines „bunk bed") ⟶ T 4	– Can you describe the situation inside the shanty? – Who has been looking after the woman in labour? – What is said about the men? – How, do you think, must Nick feel when he enters the shanty? – What happens just at that moment? – Comment on the young Indian husband in the upper bunk. Why is he smoking? – What do you make of the fact that he cut his foot badly with an axe the day before his wife's labour pains started? – How would you characterize Nick's father's reaction to the situation? – Describe Nick's behaviour while his father is preparing for the operation.
Unterrichtsschritt 3: The Operation a) Lesen ("Later when he started to operate . . ." – " . . . the basin out in the kitchen.") b) Textparaphrase und Ausdeutung unter Berücksichtigung der sprachlichen Mittel	Schüler-Lesevortrag Unterrichtsgespräch	– How does Hemingway present the actual operation itself? – Can you mention some of the facts that are not stated explicitly in the text, but are to be inferred by the reader? – What can you say about the stylistic technique that Hemingway employs at this stage in the story? – What effect does Hemingway achieve with this particular way of narrating an event? – Discuss the impact that the long and crude operation must have on Nick.

Homework: (Falls keine Doppelstunde zur Verfügung steht.)

Sum up in a few lines how Nick responds to the situation in the shanty, and comment on his part in the operation.
Compare and contrast the two fathers.
In your opinion, could the Indian father's suicide have been prevented?

T4 (to be completed in T 5)

Nick's father

in control of the situation (his hands!)

matter-of-fact

unemotional

"her screams are not important"

professional, "went to work"

Unterrichtsschritte	Unterrichtsformen	Fragestellungen
Unterrichtsschritt 1: Kurze Wiederholung der Ergebnisse	Kurzes Referieren durch Schüler	– Repeat briefly how Nick responds to the situation in the shanty, and comment on his part in the operation.
Unterrichtsschritt 2: The Discovery of the Young Indian Father's Suicide a) Lesen ("Uncle George looked at his arm . . ." – ". . . tipped the Indian's head back.") b) Paraphrase und Ausdeutung	Unterrichtsgespräch Schüler-Lesevortrag ⟶ T 4 ergänzen zu T 5	– How does Nick's father behave immediately after the operation? Discuss the doctor's feelings at this point. – What do you make of Uncle George's comment on the doctor? – Compare the doctor's words just before the discovery of the young Indian father's suicide to the reality he is confronted with immediately afterwards. What effect is achieved by this juxtaposition?
Unterrichtsschritt 3: The Two Fathers	Unterrichtsgespräch, dabei Vervollständigung des Tafelbildes T 4 zu T 5	– Let's look back on the whole scene in the shanty and compare the two fathers, Nick's father and the young Indian. – Could the Indian father's suicide have been prevented? – Where is Nick at the moment of the discovery of the suicide? – What assumptions can we make regarding the effect that the discovery of the suicide might have on Nick?
Homework: What is Nick's response to the events of the night? How do you interpret the end of the story?		

TWO FATHERS

Nick's father		The Indian husband

Nick's father

in control of the situation
(his hands!)   ⟷   nervous (smoking;
                                          cut his foot 3 days ago!)

matter-of-fact   quiet   (trying to control himself)

unemotional

"her screams are not important"   ⟷   can't stand his wife's pain

professional, "went to work" | "it all took a long time" | suffers, despairs

↓

success   ⟷   **suicide**

"just sew up the incision I made"   ⟷   cut throat
(with a jackknife!)   ⟷   (with a razor!)

↓

exalted, exhilarated   ⟷   "took it all pretty quietly"

"the doctor", "great man"

"one for the medical journal"

"these little (!) affairs"

} **pride**

↓

discovers the Indian
father's suicide   – – – – – – – – →   "an awful mess"

NICK

Unterrichtsschritte	Unterrichtsformen	Fragestellungen
Unterrichtsschritt 1: Anknüpfung an die vorangegangene Stunde	Kurzes Referieren durch Schüler	– Let's sum up in a few sentences what we said about the two fathers and Nick during and after the operation.
Unterrichtsschritt 2: The Return from the Indian Camp a) Lesen ("It was just beginning ..." bis zum Ende) b) Genaue Paraphrase	Schüler-Lesevortrag Unterrichtsgespräch	 – How does Nick's father talk to his son now, on their way back? – What does this display of concern and consideration tell us about Nick's father? – Comment on Nick's many questions. What do they indicate? – Why do you think Uncle George has absented himself? – What does Nick's last question reveal?
Unterrichtsschritt 3: The Result of Nick's Experience (Einbezug der Hausaufgabe)	Unterrichtsgespräch ⟶ T 6	– Describe the situation at the end of the story and compare it to the beginning. – Who does the end of the story focus on? – What is the result of Nick's experience?
Unterrichtsschritt 4: The Meaning of the Last Sentence of the Story (Einbezug der Hausaufgabe)	Unterrichtsgespräch	– What does Nick's assertion mean that he will never die?
Unterrichtsschritt 5: Hemingway's Language and Style in "Indian Camp" a) Discussion of the use of images and symbols b) Hemingway's technique of "cuts"	 Stillphase (evtl. als Hausaufgabe) ⟶ T 7 Gruppenarbeit (evtl. als Hausaufgabe)	 – What do we understand by "images" and "imagery"? – What do we understand by "symbols"? – Are there any symbols and is there any imagery in Hemingway's "Indian Camp"? – Go through the story again and note where there are "cuts" in the text. Examine what is said, how it is said, and what is not said. Fill in and write down in your own words the information that Hemingway has left out.

Unterrichtsschritt 6: Conclusion	Schülerstellungnahme	– How did you like this short story? – What do you think of the father-son relationship as portrayed in the short story? – Why do you think Hemingway chose an Indian camp as the setting for his story? – What aspects of the story would you like to discuss further? (e.g. What kind of "solution" is the Indian's suicide under the circumstances? Can suicide ever be a solution? etc.)

T6

cold on the water
Nick's father's arm
around Nick

↓

protection
trust, security

(unaware,
Nick is still
"in the dark")

Nick's
experience
of
human suffering
(birth + death)

The journey to the Indian camp:
darkness ——→ light
courage ——→ despair
birth ——→ death
success ——→ failure

water felt warm
Nick's father rowing
Nick opposite his father

↓

protection
trust, security

(Nick is more aware
of life forces now,
but too young to rationalize.)

T7

started off in the dark	——→	blew out his lantern, light of the shanties, lamp	——→	lamp	——→	beginning daylight	——→	the sun coming up	} light imagery

lake shore bay water, mist	——→	beach meadow wet with dew	——→	water on the stove	——→	wetness of blood birth death	——→	water of the lake	} water imagery

Unterrichtsschritte	Unterrichtsformen	Fragestellungen
Unterrichtsschritt 1: Hinführung zur Short Story „The Killers" a) Bereitstellung bzw. Reaktivierung landeskundlicher Information b) Worterklärungen (können teilweise schon vorher einfließen!)	Unterrichtsgespräch, z. T. Lehrervortrag, evtl. Einsatz von Dias oder Bildern (typische "fast food places" an Schnellstraßen) Einführung der unbekannten Vokabeln im Lehrer-Schüler-Gespräch, Tafelanschrieb der erklärten Wörter	– You know a lot about big city problems, but what do you know about small town communities in the US? – Comment on the contrast between the big cities and small towns. – What can you say about traffic connections between towns in the US? – What would you order in a roadside lunch-room?
Unterrichtsschritt 2: Textpräsentation a) Lesen (Anfang bis " . . . 'I'll have ham and eggs', the man called Al said.") b) Überprüfen des Textverständnisses (kurze Paraphrase)	– „Interpretierendes Lesen" durch den Lehrer (die Bücher der Schüler bleiben zunächst geschlossen) – Kurze Still-Lesephase – Nochmaliges Lesen durch guten Schüler Unterrichtsgespräch	 – How does this story open?
Unterrichtsschritt 3: Besprechung der „setting" und der erwähnten Personen	Unterrichtsgespräch mit begleitendem Tafelanschrieb ⟶ T 1	– Let's take a look at the setting now. Where and when does the story open? – How many persons are there in the room? Who are they? – How could we characterize the situation at this point?
Unterrichtsschritt 4: Besprechung der Sprachebene	Ergänzung des Tafelanschriebs	– What would you say about the language used in the opening of this short story?

Homework:

Read the beginning of Hemingway's short story "The Killers" again, and prepare the text
up to " . . . 'What would we do to a nigger?' "
How does the atmosphere of the beginning of the story change?
Look up the words that you don't know in a dictionary, and write them down in a
separate word list.

T1

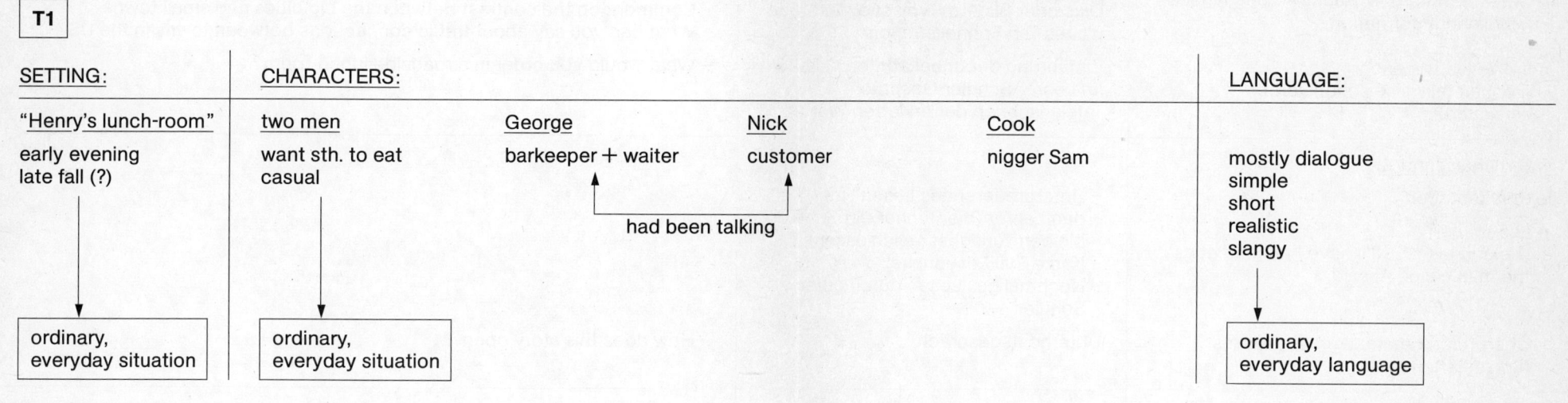

SETTING:

"Henry's lunch-room"

early evening
late fall (?)

↓

| ordinary,
| everyday situation |

CHARACTERS:

two men

want sth. to eat
casual

↓

| ordinary,
| everyday situation |

George
barkeeper + waiter

Nick
customer

↑_____↑
had been talking

Cook
nigger Sam

LANGUAGE:

mostly dialogue
simple
short
realistic
slangy

↓

| ordinary,
| everyday language |

Unterrichtsschritte	Unterrichtsformen	Fragestellungen
Unterrichtsschritt 1: Wiederholung der Ergebnisse a) Lesen (vom Anfang bis "'What would we do to a nigger?'") b) Kurze Rekapitulation von "setting, persons, atmosphere"	Schülervortrag Folie mit T 1	– Let's repeat briefly what we said about the opening of Hemingway's short story.
Unterrichtsschritt 2: Al's and Max's Strange Behaviour Überprüfen des Textverständnisses, Paraphrase des neuen Textabschnitts mit gleichzeitiger Ausdeutung (Einbezug der Hausaufgabe)	Fragend-entwickelndes Verfahren Ergänzung des Tafelanschriebs der 1. Stunde auf der Folie ⟶ T 2	– What are the two men called? How are their names revealed? – How are they described? – What strikes you about this description? – The hats, the overcoats – does this remind you of something? – Why do the men keep their gloves on? – What happens in the second passage? – What does Al mean by " . . . anything to drink", and Max by "This is a hot town"? – Comment on the behaviour of the two men. – How does Hemingway manage to create tension? – What effect does Al's and Max's behaviour have on Nick Adams and George?
Unterrichtsschritt 3: (fakultativ) Analyse der Sprache	Unterrichtsgespräch	– Looking back over the first two pages: what elements determine the development of an increasing sense of danger?
Unterrichtsschritt 4: Dialogische Präsentation des Textes	In kurzer Stillphase kennzeichnen die Schüler die jeweiligen Sprecher. Schülerlesevortrag mit verteilten Rollen.	

Homework:

Prepare the text from "George opened the slit . . ." – " . . . George looked up at the clock."
What are further steps in the development of the situation?
Draw a few lines indicating the counter, the mirror, the door, the wicket, and the
grouping of persons in the lunch-room.

T2

SETTING:	CHARACTERS:				LANGUAGE:

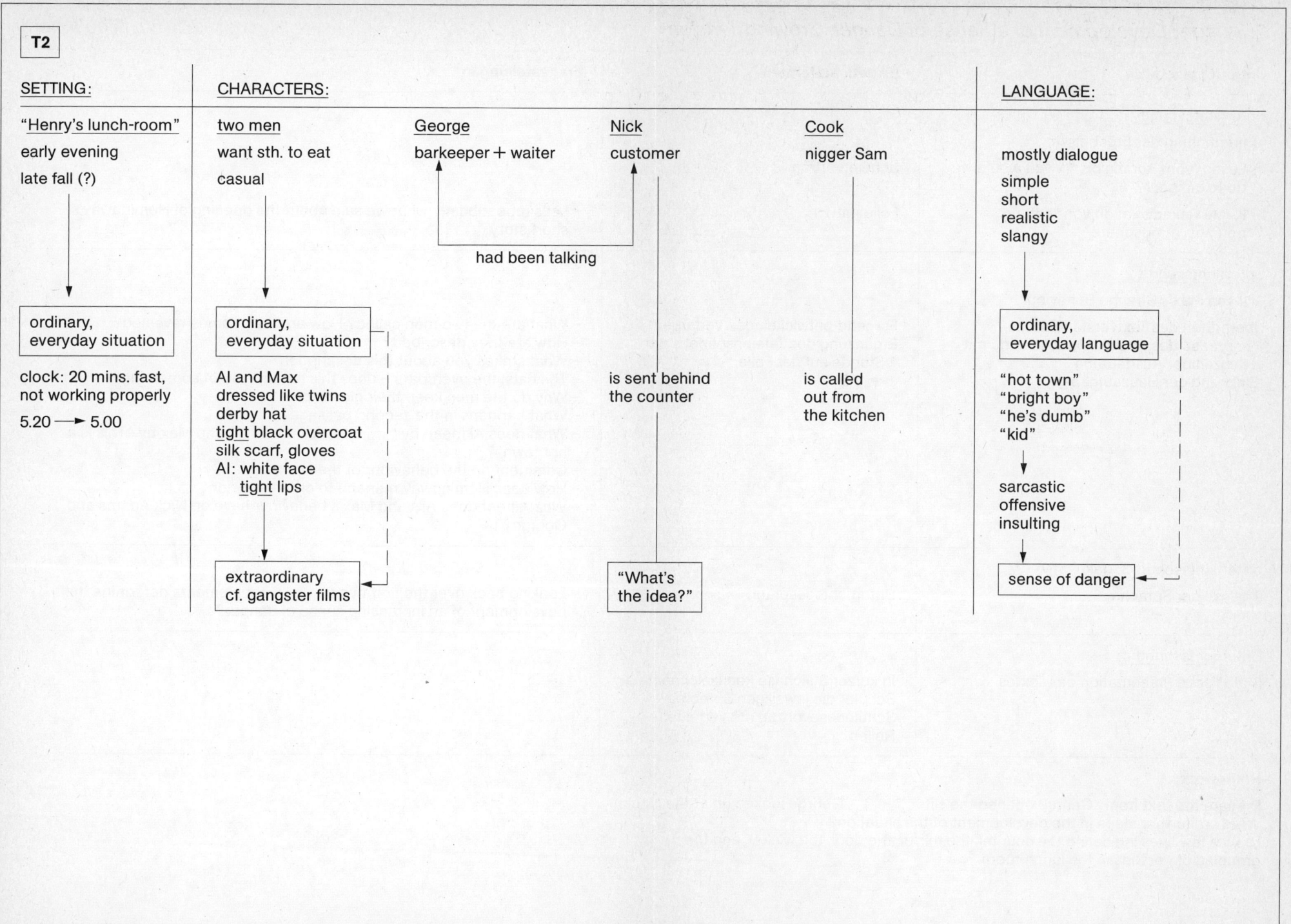

SETTING:

"Henry's lunch-room"

early evening

late fall (?)

↓

ordinary,
everyday situation

clock: 20 mins. fast,
not working properly

5.20 ⟶ 5.00

CHARACTERS:

two men

want sth. to eat

casual

↓

ordinary,
everyday situation

Al and Max
dressed like twins
derby hat
tight black overcoat
silk scarf, gloves
Al: white face
     tight lips

↓

extraordinary
cf. gangster films

George

barkeeper + waiter

↑

had been talking

Nick

customer

↑

is sent behind
the counter

"What's
the idea?"

Cook

nigger Sam

is called
out from
the kitchen

LANGUAGE:

mostly dialogue

simple
short
realistic
slangy

↓

ordinary,
everyday language

"hot town"
"bright boy"
"he's dumb"
"kid"

↓

sarcastic
offensive
insulting

↓

sense of danger

3. Stunde: Preparation for Murder

Unterrichtsschritte	Unterrichtsformen	Fragestellungen
Unterrichtsschritt 1: Überprüfen der Hausaufgabe – Kontrolle der Kenntnis einiger Vokabeln	Gezieltes Abfragen	– Who normally wears an apron and for what purpose? – What is the difference between a chair and a stool? – Do you know the British word for movies? – Give a synonym for to oblige a person. – What is a convent? – What language does the word kosher stem from, and what does it mean?
Unterrichtsschritt 2: Lesen des vorbereiteten Abschnitts ("George opened the slit . . ." – "George looked up at the clock.")	Interpretierendes Lesen durch guten Schüler	
Unterrichtsschritt 3: Further Steps in the Development of the Situation – Paraphrase und Ausdeutung des Texts – Berücksichtigung der sprachlichen Mittel	Lehrer-Schüler-Gespräch Begleitender Tafelanschrieb und Skizze des Lunchrooms (möglichst durch Schüler) → T 3 → Illustration	– What are the further steps in the development of the situation? – How does the cook respond to the gangsters' threatening behaviour? – And Nick? – Why does Al arrange the position of George and Max "like a photographer"? – Comment on Al's use of language in this passage. – How does George take the insolence and provocation? – Why does Max tell George to go to the movies more? – For what reason do Max and Al want to kill the Swede? – Can you explain Max's flippant joke about Al's having been in a "kosher convent"? – Why does George look up at the clock?

Homework: (oder Stillarbeit, falls eine Doppelstunde zur Verfügung steht)

Prepare from "George looked up at the clock" to "The two of them went out the door."
What effect is achieved by the constant references to the clock? Make a time schedule:
write down the times mentioned and note what happens on each occasion.

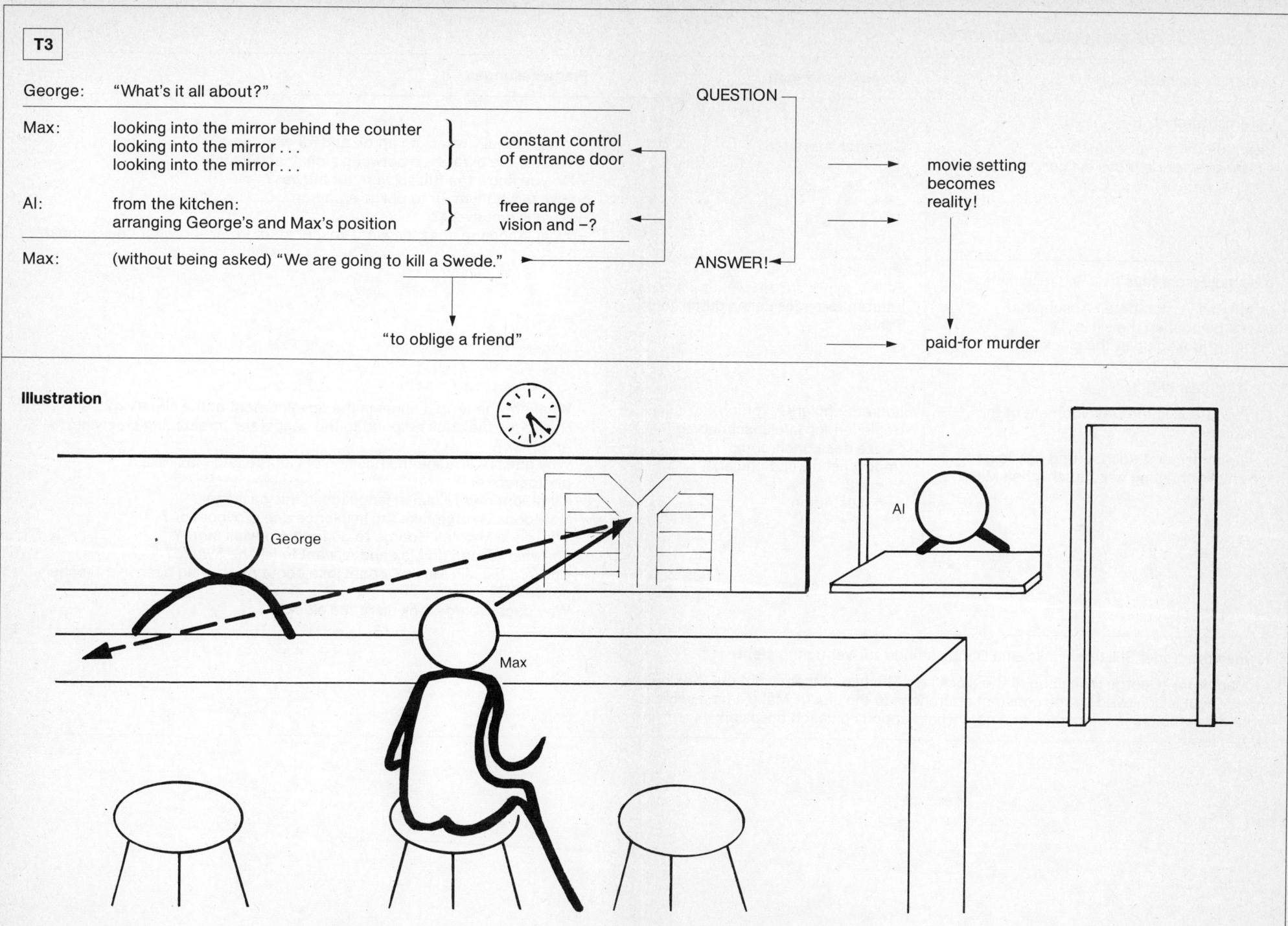

Unterrichtsschritte	Unterrichtsformen	Fragestellungen
Unterrichtsschritt 1: Lesen des vorbereiteten Abschnitts ("George looked up at the clock." – "The two of them went out the door.")	Schüler-Lesevortrag	
Unterrichtsschritt 2: Waiting for the Kill a) Kurze Paraphrase des Textabschnitts	Unterrichtsgespräch mit begleitendem Tafelanschrieb → T 4 Einbezug der von den Schülern vorbereiteten Liste der Zeitangaben im Text	– Can you give a short summary of this passage?
b) Genaue schrittweise Ausdeutung		– At what time do the killers expect Ole Andreson? – How do they prepare for the kill? – In what manner are Max's instructions given? – How does George react? – What does Max's answer to George's question "What you going to do with us afterwards?" imply? – How is tension increased? – What does George's behaviour in this situation reveal? – What effect is achieved by the constant references to time? – How is Al described now? – Describe the position Nick and the cook are in. – What is the implication in Al's question: "What about the two bright boys and the nigger?" and his comment: "You got a lot of luck."? – What does the last sentence ("The two of them went out the door.") mean for the men concerned?
Unterrichtsschritt 3: Graphische Darstellung der Spannungskurve	Ein oder mehrere Schüler skizzieren eine Spannungskurve an der Tafel.	– Let's draw a diagram indicating the curve of tension up to the point when the two killers leave the room.

Homework:

Prepare from "George watched them . . ." – "I'll go up there."
How do George, Nick, and the cook behave when the danger is over?
List the steps in the development of the short story "The Killers" up to this point, and find headings or write one sentence for each of these steps.

clock:		correct time:	
5.15	→	4.55	Al and Max enter
5.20	→	5.00	Al and Max order a meal
6.20	→	6.00	Ole Andreson expected

~6.00 → 5.40   Al's and Max's preparations   → orders to George   Tension building up

↓ George obliges (at gunpoint!)   ↓ Great tension

6.15 → 5.55   Door opens: streetcar driver enters

6.20 → 6.00   Streetcar driver leaves
2 other people

↓ G.: "He's not coming."   ↓ Tension increased
"Your friend is not going to come."

6.55 → 6.35   "We'll give him 10 mins."   ↓ T

7.05 → 6.45   "We better go"
". . . give him 5 mins."   ↓ T

7.10 → 6.50   A man comes in   ↓ T

↓

7.15 → 6.55   Al and Max leave   Tension relieved

"the time is out of joint"

Unterrichtsschritte	Unterrichtsformen	Fragestellungen
Unterrichtsschritt 1: Rückblick über den Aufbau der Geschichte	Unterrichtsgespräch und vorbereitete Folie	– Let's take a brief look at the development of the story so far, and at the construction of the story. What steps can we list?
Unterrichtsschritt 2: Textpräsentation ("George watched them . . ." – "'I'll go up there.'"	Lehrervortrag!	
Unterrichtsschritt 3: Nick's Conflict Genaue Ausdeutung des Textabschnitts	Besprechung im fragend-entwickeln-den Verfahren anhand der Leitfrage der Hausaufgabe. Begleitender Tafelanschrieb ⟶ T 5	– When the danger is over: how does George react and how does the cook react? – What attitudes do George and the cook represent respectively? – What position does Nick find himself in? – Comment on the importance of Nick's conflict, and on his decision.
Unterrichtsschritt 4: Possible Consequences of Nick's Decision	Die Schüler überlegen, wie die Geschichte weiter verlaufen könnte.	– What do we anticipate with regard to Nick's attempt to warn Ole Andreson and save his life? – How do we expect Ole Andreson to react?

Homework:

Read and prepare the text ("Outside the arc-light shone . . .") up to the end of the story.
Subdivide the passage into two parts and find a headline for each part.
How is Ole Andreson described? Comment on his behaviour.

T5

George	Nick	The Cook
"You'd better go and see Ole Andreson." ⟶	CHOICE ◄—	—— "You'd better not have anything to do with it"
		" . . . stay out"
tries to cope with the situation; keeps his head; (humane? resigned? concerned?)	involvement or evasion DECISION: "I'll go see him."	is cowardly, evasive, egotistic

Unterrichtsschritte	Unterrichtsformen	Fragestellungen
Unterrichtsschritt 1: The Outcome of Nick's Efforts a) Kontrastierung der Schülerspekulationen mit der überraschenden Haltung Ole Andresons b) Unterteilung des Schlußabschnitts	Unterrichtsgespräch	– Remember what you said in our last discussion on how we expect Ole Andreson to react? How does he react, in fact? – Which two parts did you subdivide the final passage into? – What headlines did you find for these parts?
Unterrichtsschritt 2: The Atmosphere Outside – Die Funktion der zweimaligen Straßenbeschreibung	Ein Schüler liest die entsprechende Textstelle → T 6	– At the beginning of each of the two passages (when Nick goes to Ole Andreson and when he returns from him) Hemingway gives some description of the street Nick walks up. What effect is achieved by this description?
Unterrichtsschritt 3: Nick Sees Ole Andreson a) Lesen des ersten Teils der Schlußpassage ("Outside the arc-light shone . . ." – "'Goodnight', the woman said.") b) Paraphrase und Ausdeutung des Textabschnitts	Schüler-Lesevortrag Unterrichtsgespräch mit begleiten-dem Tafelanschrieb → T 7	 – Where is Ole's room situated? (Implication?) – Give a detailed description of how Nick finds Ole Andreson in Hirsch's rooming-house when he opens the door of Ole's room. – What sort of questions does Ole ask? – Who does he expect? – Why does he keep looking at the wall? – How does he react to Nick's warning? – Why doesn't he try to run away? – What can we say then about the result of Nick's mission? – What effect do you think must Mrs Bell's comments have on Nick?
Unterrichtsschritt 4: (fakultativ) Irritating, Confusing Elements in the Story	Unterrichtsgespräch → T 8	– What do you make of Nick's mistaking Mrs Bell's identity? – Are there further examples of similarly confusing identities or seeming contradictions? (→ T 8) – Why do you think Hemingway includes these confusing elements?

Homework:

1. What is the result of Nick's experience in this story?
2. How would you depict the development of this story in a dramatic curve? (Make a diagram.)

T6

<u>outside:</u>

arc lights   ⟶   cold, glaring   ⎫

bare branches   ⟶   barren, desolate ⎬   outlines only

car tracks   ⟶   ? anonymous   ⎭   ↓

                                                     desolate atmosphere

---

T7

Hirsch's rooming-house:

Ole Andreson, heavyweight prize-fighter

"Who is it?"	lying on bed with clothes on	⎫
	not looking at Nick	
"What was it?"	looking at the wall	
"There isn't anything I can do about it"	talking to the wall (flat voice)	⎬ submits to his fate
"There ain't anything to do"		
"There ain't anything to do"		
"There ain't anything to do"		
"I got in wrong"		⎭
↓		

Nick's attempt to help   "an awfully nice man"

(and save human life) is futile!   beaten-up face ⟷ "gentle"

T8

CONTRADICTIONS:

"Hirsch's rooming-house"	but:	Mrs Bell looks after it
"Henry's lunch-room"	but:	George runs it
lunch-counter	but:	formerly a saloon
Ole A., a heavyweight prize-fighter	but:	not fighting; submitting!
beaten-up face	but:	"gentle", "awfully nice"
two men: "vaudeville team"	but:	gangsters, killers
clock	but:	incorrect time (cf. Hamlet: "the time is out of joint")

⟵   ⟶

CONTRASTS

APPEARANCE VS. REALITY

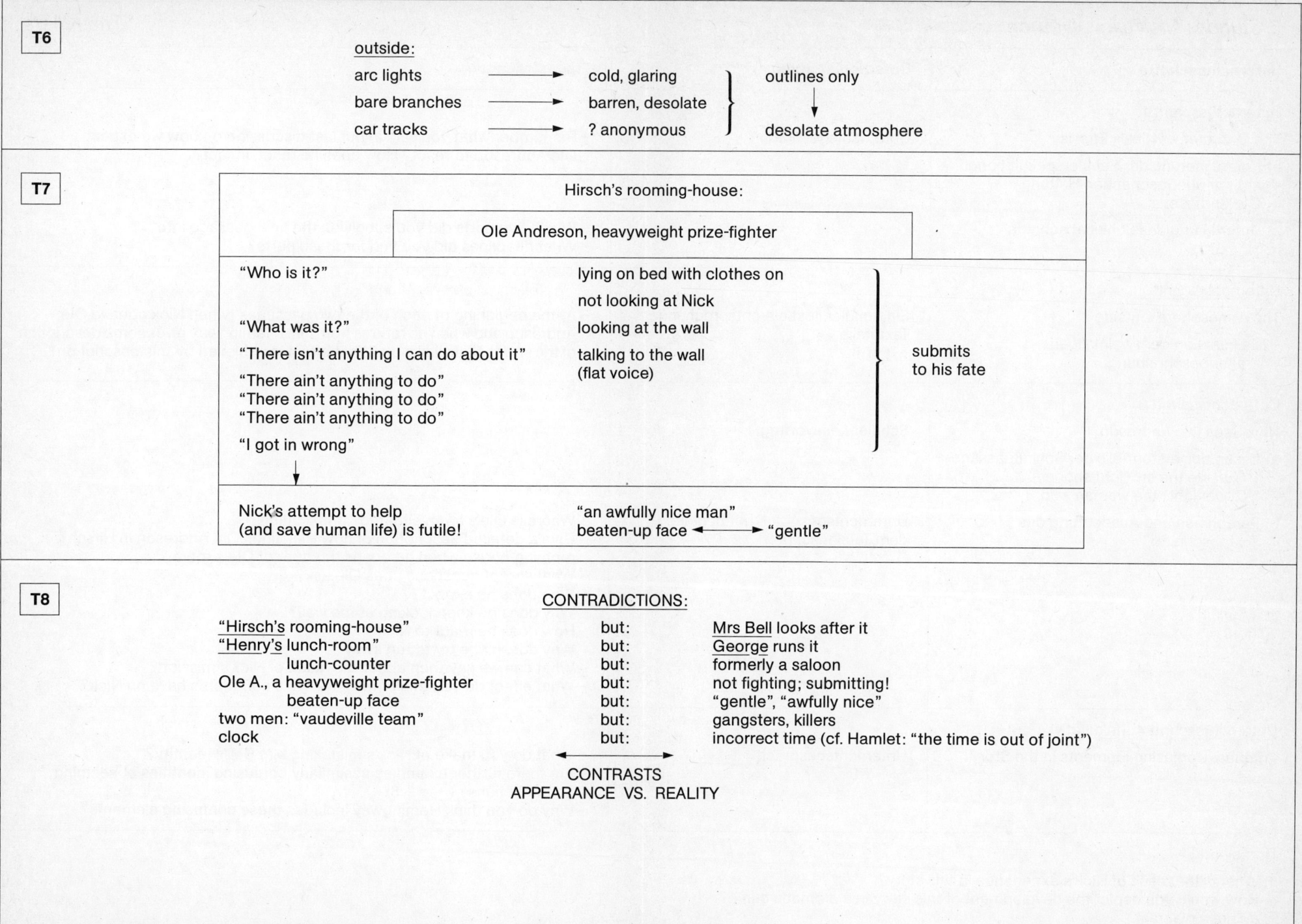

Unterrichtsschritte	Unterrichtsformen	Fragestellungen
Unterrichtsschritt 1: The Result of Nick's Experience a) Einstieg b) Lesen des letzten Abschnitts (von "Nick walked up the dark street...") c) Paraphrase und Ausdeutung des Schlußteils (Einbezug der Hausaufgabe)	 Lehrer-Leitfrage Schüler-Lesevortrag Unterrichtsgespräch mit begleiten-dem Tafelanschrieb ⟶ T 9	 – The story could have ended at "'Goodnight', the woman said." Why do you think Hemingway added the last passage? – What is the result of Nick's experience? – How does he talk about it? – What does Nick's manner of talking about his experience reveal about his feelings? – Can you imagine what must go through Nick's mind when he sees George wiping the counter with a towel? – How do George's comments and his behaviour characterize him?
Unterrichtsschritt 2: Nick's Lesson – Auswertung der ganzen Short Story „The Killers". Kennzeichnung der Geschichte als „initiation story"	 Unterrichtsgespräch	– What lesson does Nick learn? – Why does Nick leave the town in the end? – Why doesn't George want to leave? – Does Nick's leaving the town change anything? – What do you think will happen to Nick when he follows the car tracks and gets to some other town?
Unterrichtsschritt 3: Analyse des Gesamtaufbaus der Kurzgeschichte (Einbezug der Hausaufgabe)	Unterrichtsgespräch ⟶ T 10	

T9

The Result of Nick's Experience

Nick:

"He (Ole A.) won't go out . . ."   Frustration! (Nick's involvement proved futile)

"I guess they will" (kill him)   Acceptance of brutal reality?

"It's an awful thing"   Moved, shocked

"I wonder what he did"   Nick can't help thinking of Ole Andreson

"I'm going to get out of this town!"   Attempt to run away
                                          from incomprehensible
"I can't stand it . . ."   reality,
                                          (from evil in this world)
"It's too damned awful"

Nick Adams is learning a lesson (about an aspect of life that he did not know before)

→ INITIATION STORY

George:

"You better not think about it"   but: Nick <u>does</u> think about it!

T10

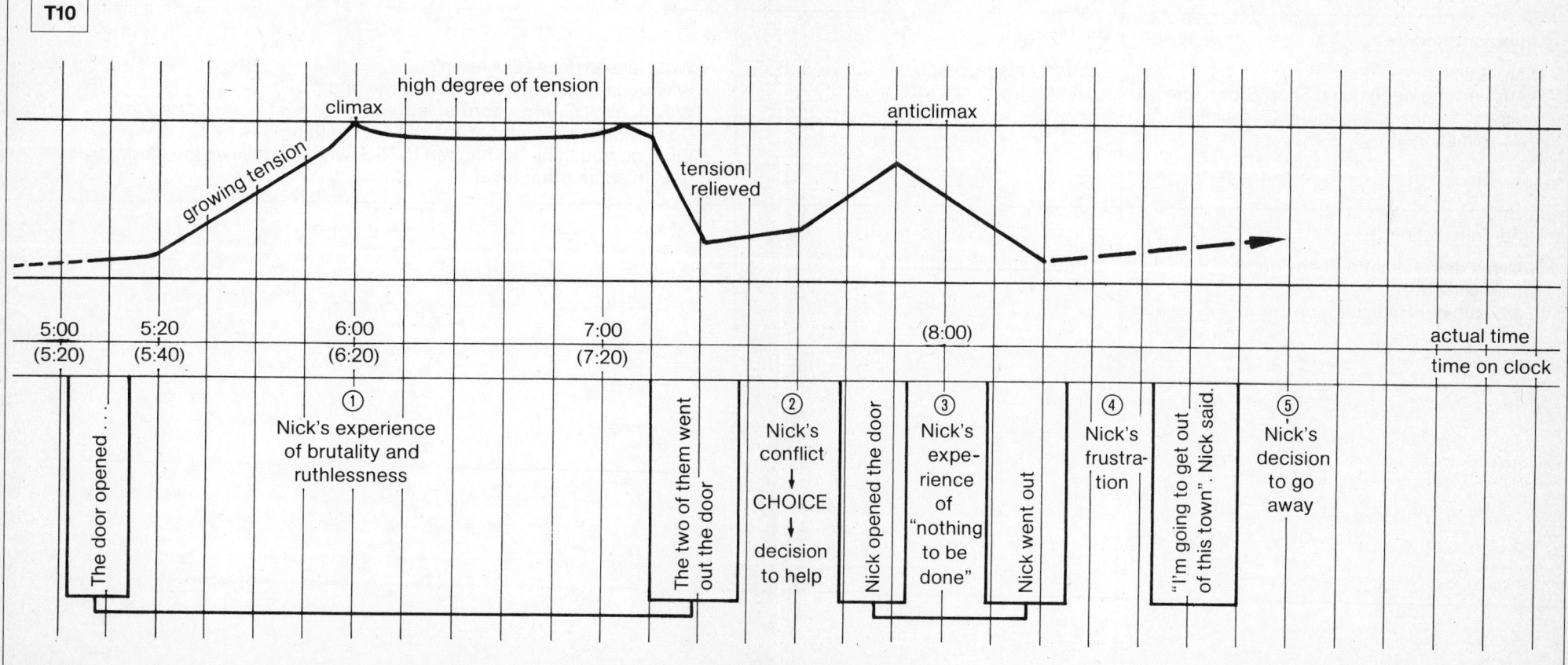

Unterrichtsschritte	Unterrichtsformen	Fragestellungen
Unterrichtsschritt 1: Hinführung zur Short Story „The Battler" Bereitstellen bzw. Reaktivierung landeskundlicher Informationen	Unterrichtsgespräch, evtl. Zeigen von Anschauungsmaterial	– Do you remember seeing any films with tramps in them? – How did those tramps travel? – How dangerous was it to climb onto and travel on a freight train? – Do you know what might have happened to such tramps? – What, do you think, was their reason for tramping? – How (and why) do people "tramp" nowadays?
Unterrichtsschritt 2: Textpräsentation des Anfangs a) Lesen (Anfang bis " . . . nearly to Mancelona.") b) Überprüfen einiger für das Verständnis wichtiger Vokabeln c) Überprüfen des Textverständnisses	Schüler-Lesevortrag Vokabelkontrolle durch den Lehrer Inhaltliche Zusammenfassung durch einen oder mehrere Schüler	– Can you sum up in a sentence or two what we get to know in the opening passage?
Unterrichtsschritt 3: Nick Busted off the Freight Train a) Besprechung der „setting" b) Beschreibung Nicks	Unterrichtsgespräch mit begleitendem Tafelanschrieb ——► T 1 Tafelbild T 1 ergänzen	– Where is Nick when he finds himself knocked off the freight train? Describe his surroundings. – What can we say about the setting then? – Do we know anything about Nick's destination? – Let's take a closer look at Nick now. What do we learn about him? – Why is he so angry? – Comment on the line "What a lousy kid thing to have done".

Homework: (falls keine Doppelstunde zur Verfügung steht)

1. Read the first part of the story again. (Up to " . . . walked into the fire-light.")
2. Which words are used most often in this opening part?
3. Why do you think they are used so often?
4. Draw a rough sketch of the scene.

T1

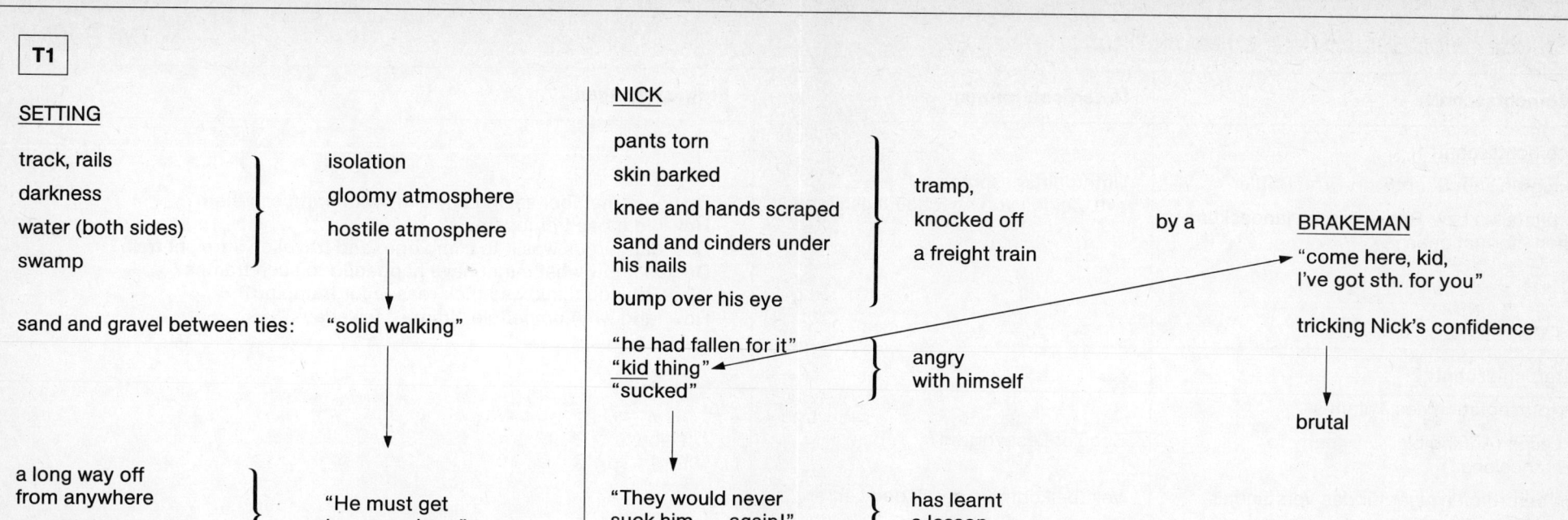

SETTING

track, rails ⎫
darkness ⎬ isolation
water (both sides) ⎭ gloomy atmosphere
swamp hostile atmosphere

sand and gravel between ties: "solid walking"

a long way off ⎫
from anywhere ⎬ "He must get
causeway through ⎭ to somewhere"
the swamp

NICK

pants torn ⎫
skin barked ⎬ tramp,
knee and hands scraped ⎬ knocked off by a
sand and cinders under ⎬ a freight train
his nails ⎭
bump over his eye

"he had fallen for it" ⎫
"kid thing" ⎬ angry
"sucked" ⎭ with himself

"They would never ⎫ has learnt
suck him . . . again!" ⎭ a lesson

BRAKEMAN

"come here, kid,
I've got sth. for you"

tricking Nick's confidence

brutal

2. Stunde: Hiking Along the Track

Unterrichtsschritte	Unterrichtsformen	Fragestellungen
Unterrichtsschritt 1: Wiederholung der Ergebnisse a) Kurze Rekapitulation des Anfangs b) Lesen (bis "...walked into the fire-light.")	Ergebniszusammenfassung durch einen Schüler Schüler-Lesevortrag	– Can you briefly recapitulate the situation at the beginning?
Unterrichtsschritt 2: Nick Hiking Along the Track a) Paraphrase und begleitende Ausdeutung. Sprachliche Beobachtungen fließen mit ein. b) Illustration der Situation	Unterrichtsgespräch Tafelanschrieb ⟶ T 2 als Ergänzung von T 1 (T 1 eventuell auf Folie) Skizzierung der Situation (Tafelbild oder Folie) ⟶ T 3	– What does Nick do after he has cleaned himself and washed his wounds? – How is his hiking described? – Did you notice which words are mentioned most often? – Why do you think Hemingway repeats the words "track" and "swamp" so often? – How does the author intensify a sense of danger? – What does the unexpected sight of a fire off the track mean for Nick? – How does Nick approach the fire? – Can you illustrate on the board (or on a transparency) the layout of the situation described?

Homework:

Read and prepare the text from "The man sat there..." – "...She never speeds up'")
Pay particular attention to Ad Francis' reactions.
Note which words keep recurring in this passage that might be called keywords.

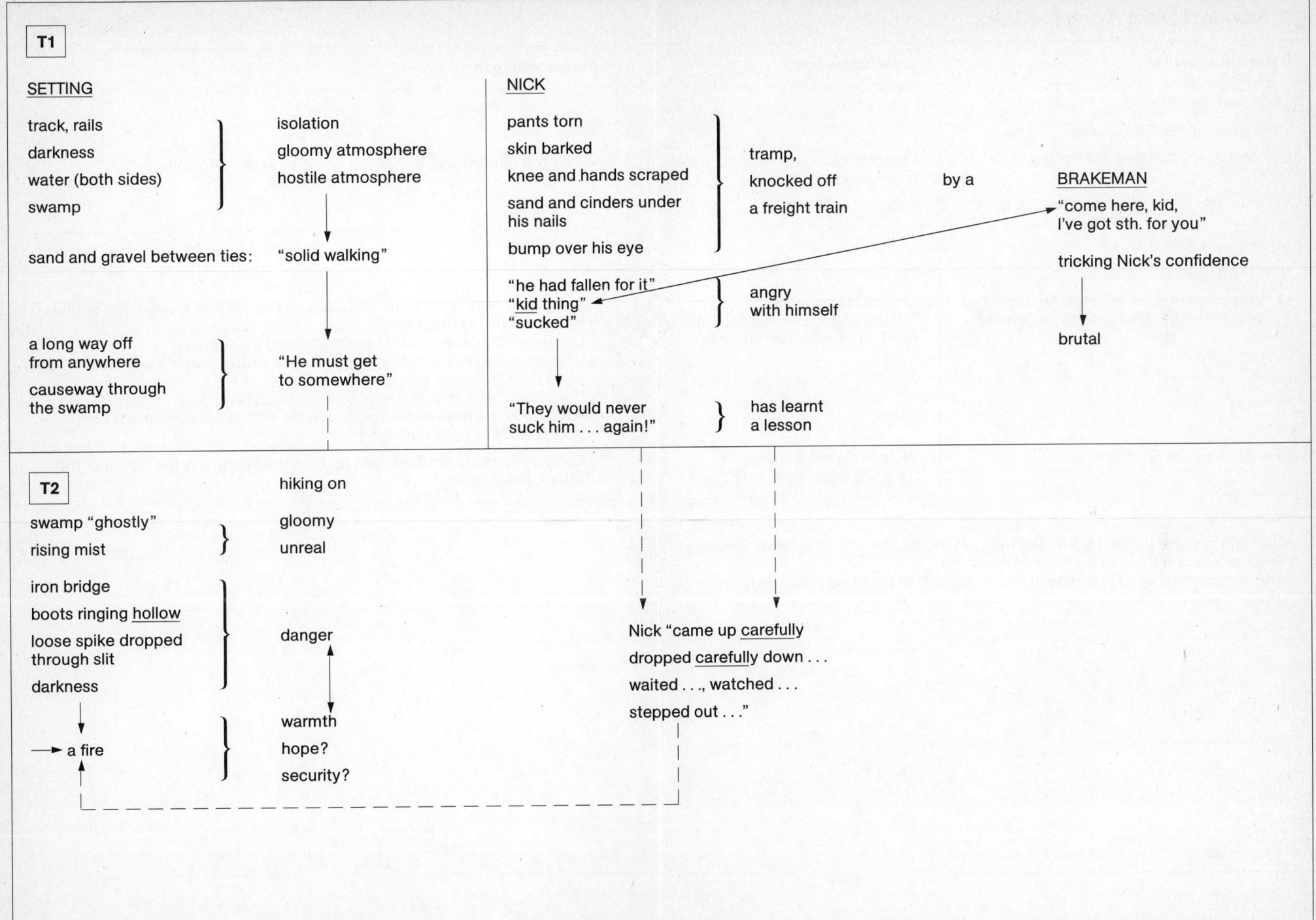

T1

SETTING

track, rails   } isolation
darkness   gloomy atmosphere
water (both sides)   hostile atmosphere
swamp

sand and gravel between ties: "solid walking"

a long way off
from anywhere   } "He must get
causeway through   to somewhere"
the swamp

NICK

pants torn   }
skin barked   tramp,
knee and hands scraped knocked off   by a   BRAKEMAN
sand and cinders under a freight train   "come here, kid,
his nails   I've got sth. for you"
bump over his eye

"he had fallen for it" }   tricking Nick's confidence
"kid thing"   angry
"sucked"   with himself   brutal

"They would never   } has learnt
suck him . . . again!"   a lesson

T2

swamp "ghostly"   } hiking on
rising mist   gloomy
                       unreal

iron bridge   }
boots ringing hollow
loose spike dropped   danger
through slit
darkness

a fire   }
                       warmth
                       hope?
                       security?

Nick "came up carefully
dropped carefully down . . .
waited . . ., watched . . .
stepped out . . ."

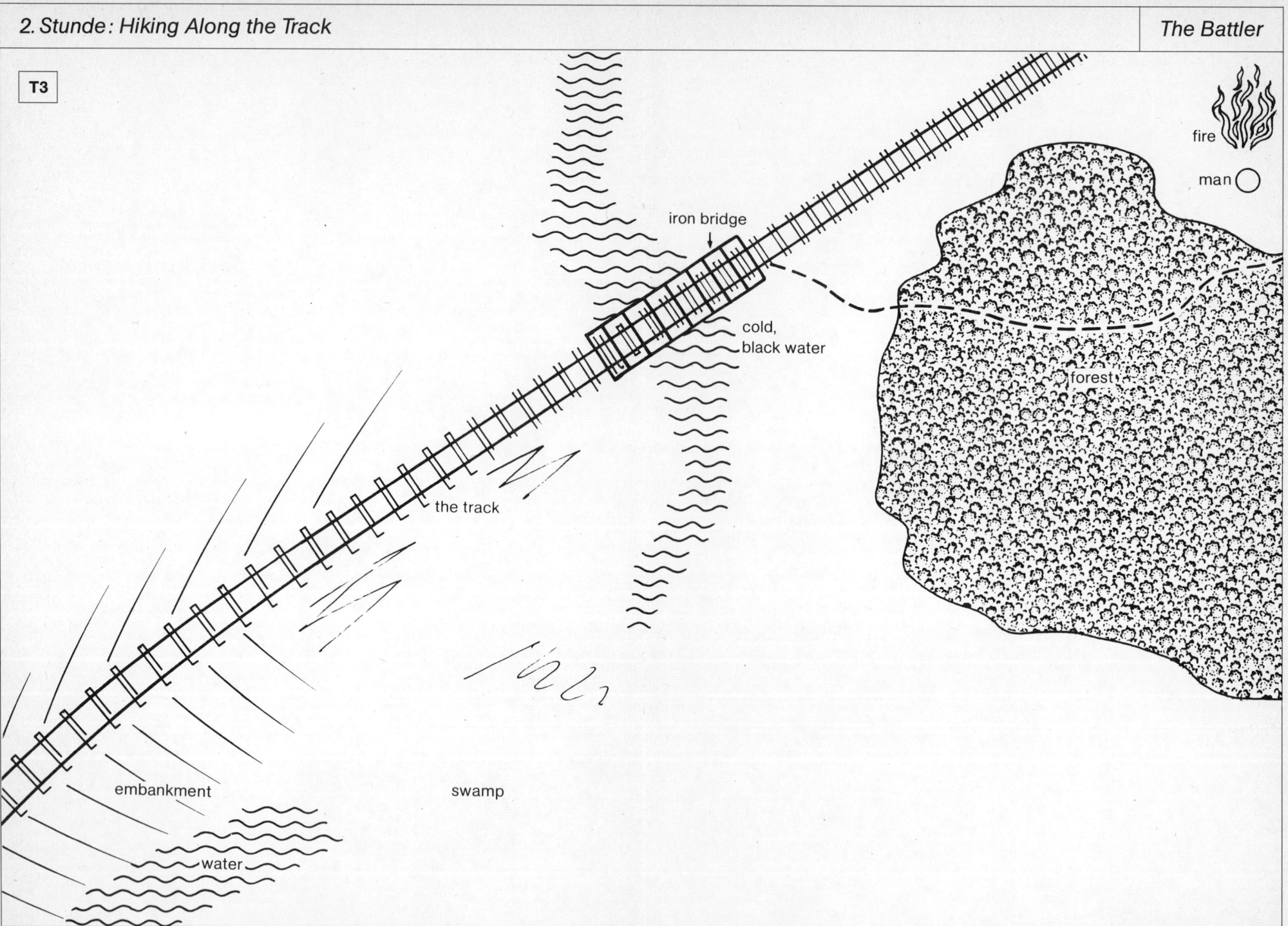

T3

fire

man

iron bridge

cold,
black water

forest

the track

embankment

swamp

water

Unterrichtsschritte	Unterrichtsformen	Fragestellungen
Unterrichtsschritt 1: a) Kurzes Anknüpfen an die vorige Stunde b) Knappe Vokabelüberprüfung c) Lesen ("The man sat there . . ." – "'She never speeds up!'")	Ergebniszusammenfassung durch einen oder mehrere Schüler Vokabelkontrolle durch Lehrer Schüler-Lesevortrag	
Unterrichtsschritt 2: Nick and the Man by the Fire – Genaue Textparaphrase mit begleitender Ausdeutung.	Unterrichtsgespräch mit begleitendem Tafelanschrieb ⟶ T 4	– Comment on the reaction of the man sitting by the fire when Nick suddenly steps up to him from behind. – How does the man welcome Nick? – What is the man's primary interest? – What advice does the man give Nick and how does the boy take this advice? – How would you characterize the man by the fire judging from his first sentences? – Describe the man's outward appearance and the effect it has on Nick. – What do we learn about the man's past? – What does the man claim as the reason for his former success as a boxer? – How do you think Nick feels when he is made to feel the boxer's pulse? – Which words keep recurring in this passage that might be called keywords?
Unterrichtsschritt 3: Dialogischer Vortrag der Textstelle	Zwei Schüler übernehmen die Rollen von Ad und Nick, ein weiterer Schüler liest die Brückentexte	

Homework:

Read and prepare from "A man dropped down . . ." – " . . . dropped the blackjack on the grass."
What effect does Bugs' arrival on the scene have on Nick?
Try and draw a dramatic curve (a curve showing the increasing tension) for the passage describing the bread episode.

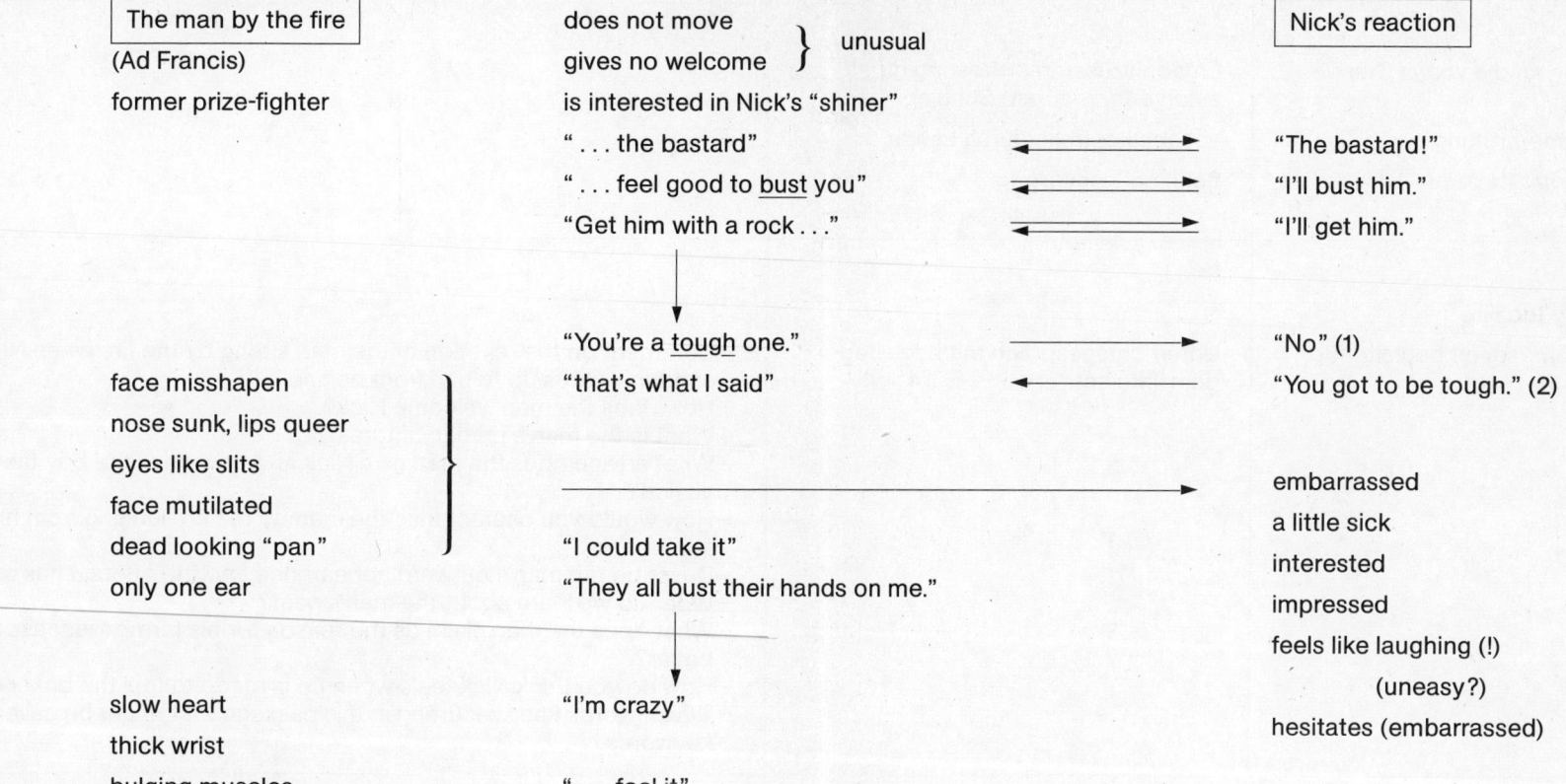

The man by the fire
(Ad Francis)
former prize-fighter

does not move
gives no welcome } unusual
is interested in Nick's "shiner"
" . . . the bastard" ⟶ "The bastard!"
" . . . feel good to bust you" ⟶ "I'll bust him."
"Get him with a rock . . ." ⟶ "I'll get him."

"You're a tough one." ⟶ "No" (1)
"that's what I said" ⟵ "You got to be tough." (2)

face misshapen
nose sunk, lips queer
eyes like slits
face mutilated
dead looking "pan"
only one ear

⟶ embarrassed
a little sick
interested
impressed
feels like laughing (!)
(uneasy?)

"I could take it"
"They all bust their hands on me."

hesitates (embarrassed)

slow heart
thick wrist
bulging muscles

"I'm crazy"

" . . . feel it"

Nick's reaction

Unterrichtsschritte	Unterrichtsformen	Fragestellungen
Unterrichtsschritt 1: Textpräsentation a) Anknüpfen an die vorige Stunde b) Lesen ("A man dropped down . . ." – " . . . blackjack on the grass.")	Kurze inhaltliche Wiederholung durch einen Schüler Schüler-Lesevortrag (3 Schüler übernehmen die Sprechrollen, ein vierter liest den Zwischentext.)	
Unterrichtsschritt 2: The Arrival of Bugs	Unterrichtsgespräch mit Tafelanschrieb ⟶ T 5	– Where has Bugs come from? – How is he described? – How does his behaviour compare with Ad's? – What effect does Bugs' arrival on the scene have on Nick? – How would you characterize the situation when Bugs starts preparing the food?
Unterrichtsschritt 3: The Bread Episode	Kurze graphische Veranschaulichung der Situation ⟶ T 6	– At which point does the seemingly sociable and friendly atmosphere begin to change? – Is Nick aware of this? – Where is Nick's main attention? – List the steps that gradually increase the tension. – Why does Bugs use Ad's full name when offering him a slice of bread? – How much sense do Ad's accusations make, when he finally attacks Nick? – Can you imagine how Nick feels in this situation? – What is the implication of Ad's repeated use of the swearword "bastard"? – At which point is Nick in real danger? – Describe the moment of greatest tension, the climax of this episode.
Unterrichtsschritt 4: Erarbeitung einer Spannungskurve	Schüler halten Spannungskurve an der Tafel fest, dann evtl. auf Folie ⟶ T 7	– Let's draw a "dramatic curve" (a curve showing the increasing tension) for the passage that we've just discussed.

Homework:

Prepare from "The little man lay there . . ." – " . . . looked childish in repose."
What made Ad Francis crazy? Give a brief written answer to this question.

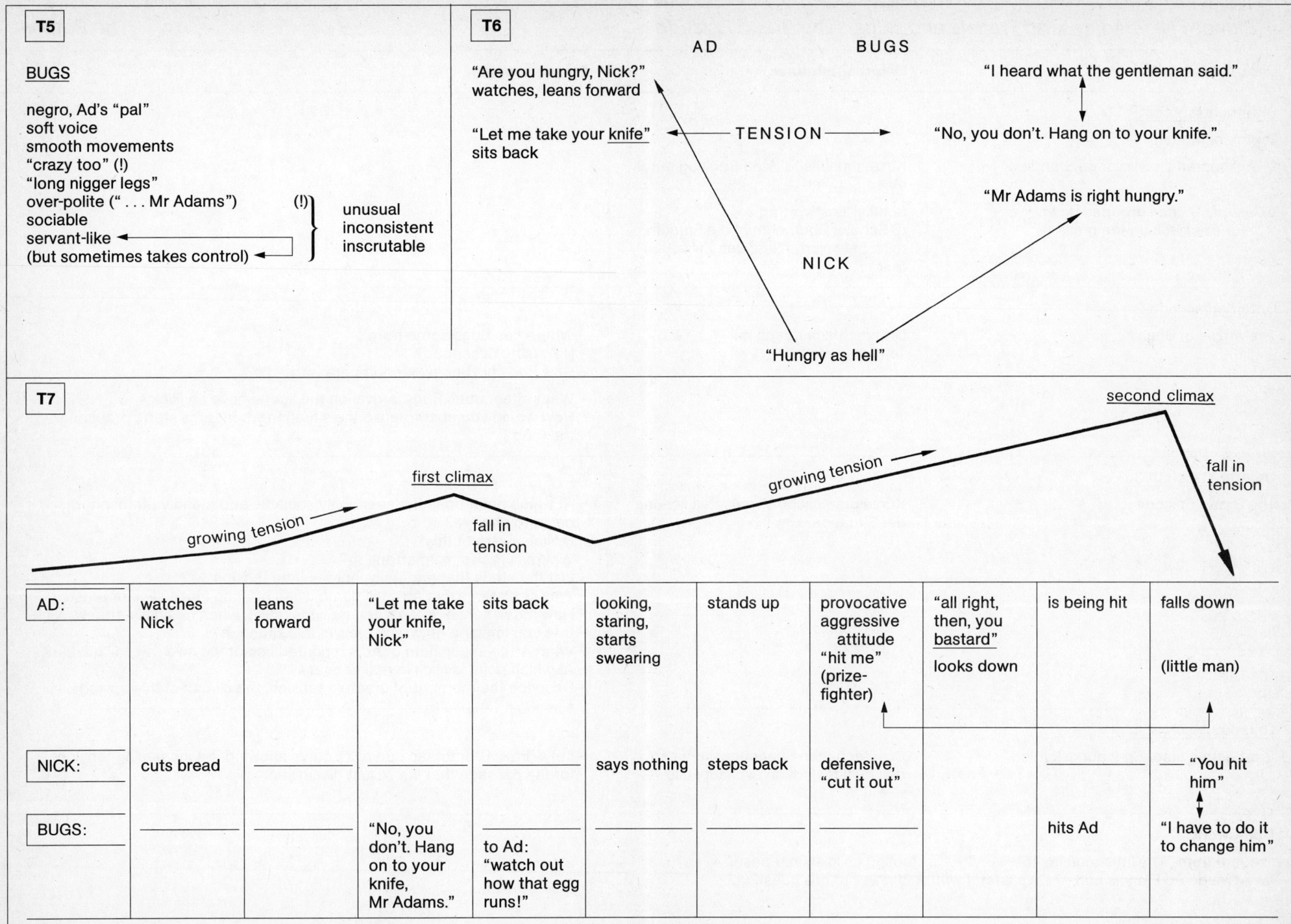

Unterrichtsschritte	Unterrichtsformen	Fragestellungen
Unterrichtsschritt 1: Textpräsentation a) Anknüpfen an die zuletzt behandelte Szene b) Zusammenfassung des vorbereiteten Textabschnitts c) Lesen ("The little man lay there . . ." – " . . . looked childish in repose.")	Schüler fassen das Gespräch zwischen Nick und Bugs zusammen Schüler-Lesevortrag	
Unterrichtsschritt 2: Bug's Behaviour After Knocking Ad out	Unterrichtsgespräch	– What can you say about the Negro's behaviour after he has knocked Ad out? – How do you imagine Nick feels at this moment? – Do you accept the explanation that Bugs gives, smiling, about the reason why he knocked Ad down?
Unterrichtsschritt 3: Talking About Ad Besprechung unter Miteinbeziehung der Hausaufgabe.	Unterrichtsgespräch mit begleitendem Tafelanschrieb ⟶ T 8 ⟶ T 9	– Comment on the two reasons that Bugs gives for Ad's craziness. – What do you think of the way the Negro talks about Ad's past (sipping his coffee!)? – How do you interpret Ad's strange love story? – How did Ad and Bugs meet? – What was the Negro in jail for? – Why did he decide to stay with Ad after his prison sentence was over? – What do you think of Bugs' comments? – Comment on the kind of answers that Nick gets to his questions. – Let's write down some of the confusing contradictions / contrasting facts.

Homework:

Read the end of the short story again.
What, in your opinion, is the meaning of the last three lines?
(What does the track stand for?)
Looking back over the whole short story: into how many parts could we divide the story?

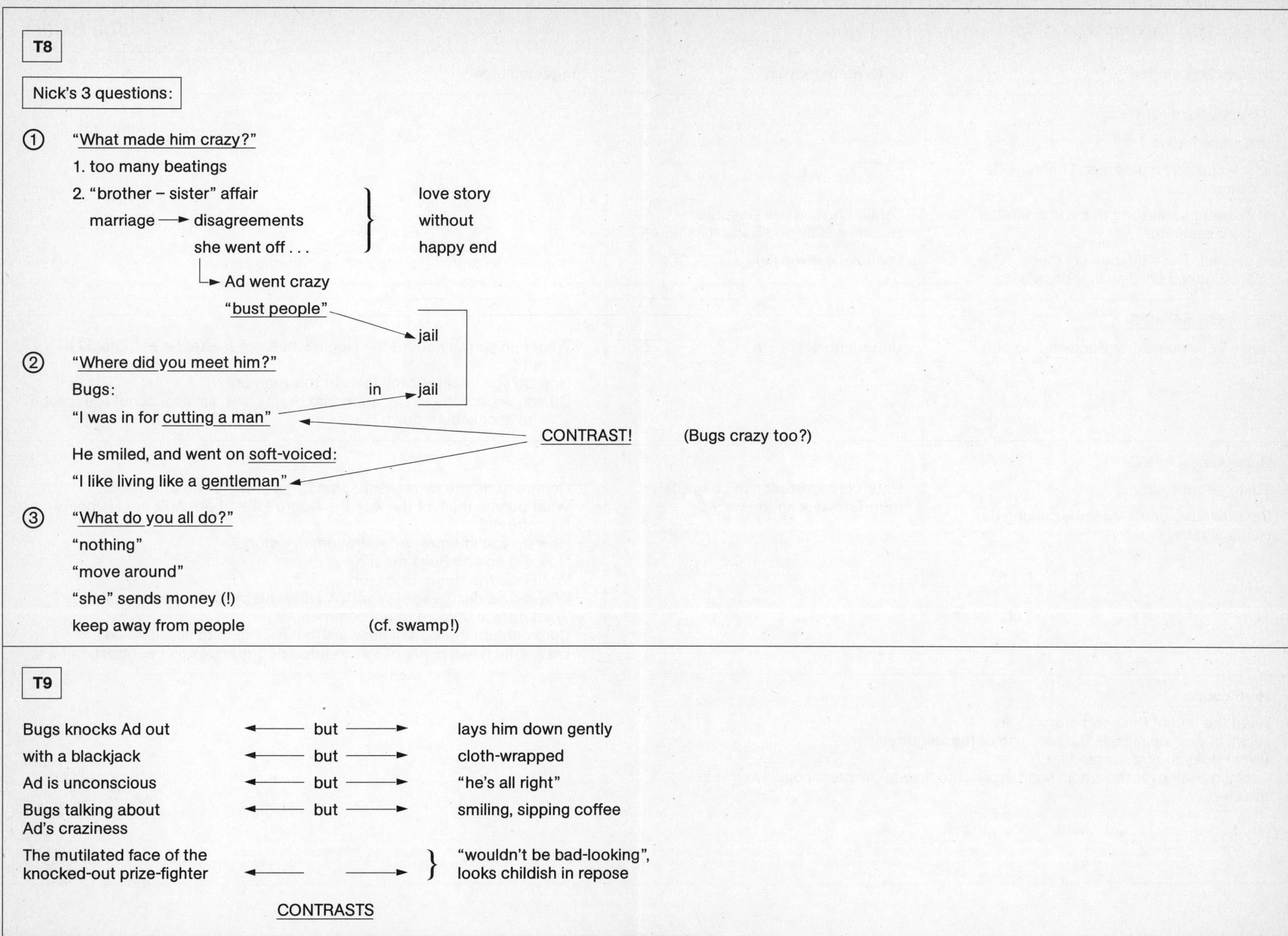

T8

Nick's 3 questions:

① "What made him crazy?"

1. too many beatings
2. "brother – sister" affair

marriage → disagreements

she went off . . .

↳ Ad went crazy

} love story / without / happy end

"bust people" → jail

② "Where did you meet him?"

Bugs: in → jail

"I was in for cutting a man"

He smiled, and went on soft-voiced:

"I like living like a gentleman"

CONTRAST!   (Bugs crazy too?)

③ "What do you all do?"

"nothing"

"move around"

"she" sends money (!)

keep away from people   (cf. swamp!)

T9

Bugs knocks Ad out	←— but —→	lays him down gently
with a blackjack	←— but —→	cloth-wrapped
Ad is unconscious	←— but —→	"he's all right"
Bugs talking about Ad's craziness	←— but —→	smiling, sipping coffee
The mutilated face of the knocked-out prize-fighter	←— —→	} "wouldn't be bad-looking", looks childish in repose

CONTRASTS

Unterrichtsschritte	Unterrichtsformen	Fragestellungen
Unterrichtsschritt 1: Kurze Anknüpfung an die vorangegangene Stunde	Zusammenfassung durch einen Schüler, evtl. Schüler-Lesevortrag	
Unterrichtsschritt 2: Nick Returns to the Track and Moves on – Paraphrase und Ausdeutung des Schluß-abschnitts	Unterrichtsgespräch	– How is Nick made to leave the scene? – How sincere do you consider Bugs' politeness? – Which way does Nick go? – What does the end mean? – Can you interpret the final sentence?
Unterrichtsschritt 3: The Construction of the Short Story	Unterrichtsgespräch	– Looking back over the whole story what can we say about the construction of "The Battler"? (How many parts? Compare beginning and end.)
Unterrichtsschritt 4: The Meaning of Hemingway's Short Story "The Battler" a) The meaning of the setting b) The meaning of Nick's journey c) The result of Nick's experience d) Hemingway's view of life in "The Battler"	Unterrichtsgespräch → T 10 Schülerorientiertes Unterrichts-gespräch Diskussion, die vor allem Schüler-reaktionen herauslocken soll → T 11 (1)	– What does the track symbolize? – What about the swamp, the forest, the hills, the fire, etc? – Why is Nick a tramp? – What does he expect to find on his journey? – What can we say about the reality that Nick is confronted with, however? – Let's sum up what we know about Ad and Bugs. – Are there any possible parallels between Ad and Nick? – Who does the title "The Battler" refer to? – What has Nick learnt from his meeting with the battler? – What is different for him now? – How does Hemingway present life in this story? – Do you find the story plausible? – What is lacking almost completely? – Can you define the main theme of the story?

Unterrichtsschritt 5: Hemingway's Language and Style in "The Battler"	→ T 11 (2) 3 possible student projects	– How would you characterize Hemingway's language and style in "The Battler"? 1. See how Hemingway manages the dialogue form. 2. Find out where in the text of the short story there is explicit mention or description of the characters' emotional reactions. 3. Study Hemingway's use of alliteration in this story. (Pay particular attention to words beginning with "b".)
Unterrichtsschritt 6: Weiterführende Fragestellungen a) Besprechung typischer Merkmale einer Short Story b) Möglichkeit von Verknüpfungen mit anderen Short Stories c) Anregung zu „creative writing"	 Unterrichtsgespräch Unterrichtsgespräch Schüler schreiben ihre eigene Fortsetzung	 – Let's try and sum up what might be considered typical characteristics of a short story. – Compare Nick's experience in "The Battler" with the one he has in "The Killers". – Write your own Nick Adams story. Describe what happens to Nick on his way. Find your own title.

T10

mutilated, misshapen
"tough", "busted", "took it"
prize-fighter, battler
former prisoner
took too many beatings
crazy

AD

on the move
keeping away from people
no home
tramp

beaten-up existence

interdependent

negro, polite, glib
gentle, soft, smooth
former prisoner
takes care of Ad
but: no real feeling,
   no genuine compassion
lives on Ad's money like
   a "gentleman"
crazy?

BUGS

on the move
keeping away from people
no home
tramp

ambiguous existence

bruised
scraped hands and leg
black eye etc.
beaten up ("busted")

NICK

on the move
no home
tramp

learning from experience

searching existence?

T11

Hemingway's View of Life in "The Battler"

harsh, unfriendly setting
realistic
episode showing hostile, ugly,
   brutal aspects of life
unromantic, hard,
no beauty, no love
a "man's world", but questionable

Hemingway's Style in "The Battler"

factual description
realistic
dialogue (simple, colloquial,
partly slang)
repetitions
alliterations

1. Stunde: The Bombing of Tortosa

Unterrichtsschritte	Unterrichtsformen	Fragestellungen
1. Unterrichtsschritt: The Spanish Civil War – causes – the two sides – course of the war – foreign intervention – outcome of the war	Schüler-Kurzreferat Folie oder handout → T 1	
2. Unterrichtsschritt: Hemingway's Engagement in the Spanish Civil War	Lehrerhinweise	

3. Unterrichtsschritt:
The Bombing of Tortosa
a) Lesen
   in drei Abschnitten
 	
b) Besprechung des Kriegsberichts
   (Einbeziehung der Leitfragen der Hausaufgabe)
 	
c) Kennzeichnung der Stilmittel
	Schüler-Lesevortrag
	
	Unterrichtsgespräch
	
	Unterrichtsgespräch
		– What bombings are described in the first two paragraphs of the dispatch?
		– Comment on the way these two bombings are carried out.
		– What types and makes of planes are mentioned? Do the names tell you anything?
		– Why is the war correspondent heading for the front?
		
		– Comment on the style in which this war report is written. (Is this what you would have expected of a typical war report? If not, in what respect does it differ?)

Homework:

Read Hemingway's short story "Old Man at the Bridge" which is set in the Spanish Civil War.
– What is the basic difference between Hemingway's war report and his short story? (Content? Form?)
– What situation is described at the opening of the short story?
– What do we learn about the narrator? And what about the old man?

T1

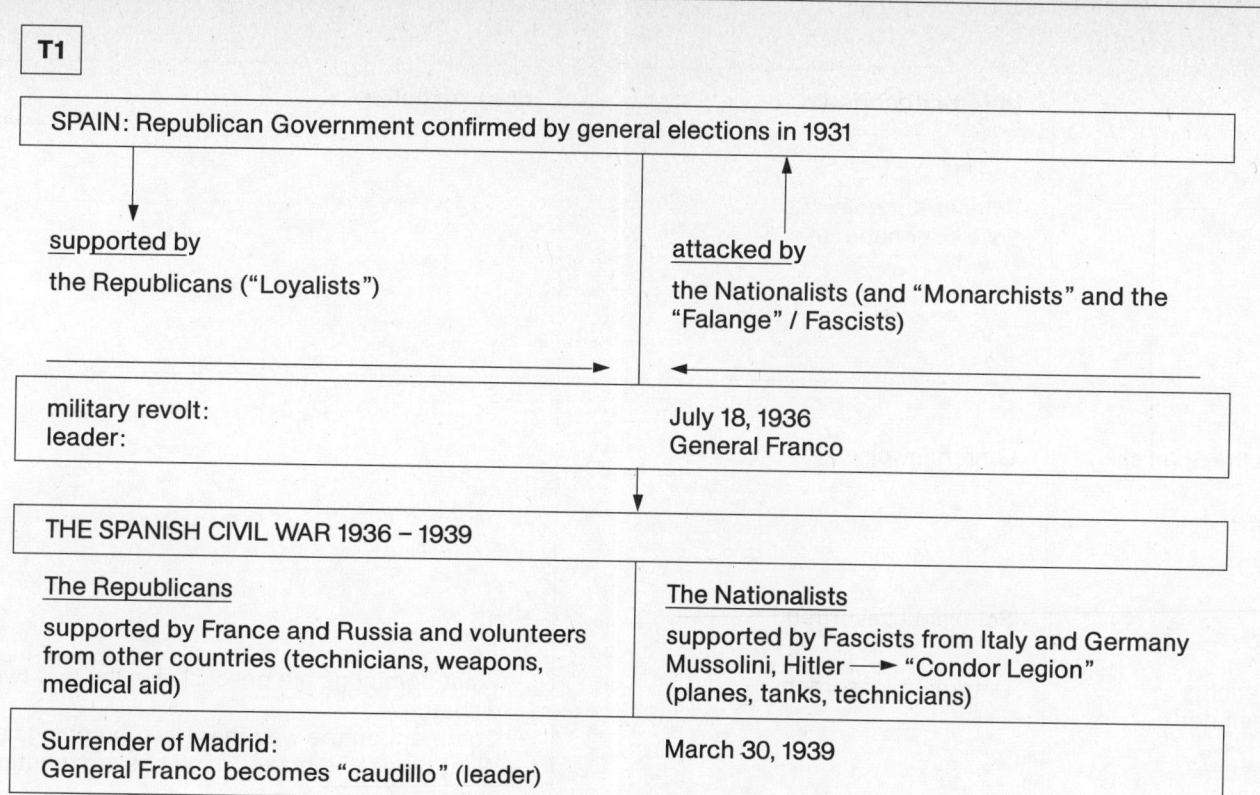

SPAIN: Republican Government confirmed by general elections in 1931

supported by
the Republicans ("Loyalists")

attacked by
the Nationalists (and "Monarchists" and the "Falange" / Fascists)

military revolt:
leader:

July 18, 1936
General Franco

THE SPANISH CIVIL WAR 1936 – 1939

The Republicans

supported by France and Russia and volunteers from other countries (technicians, weapons, medical aid)

The Nationalists

supported by Fascists from Italy and Germany Mussolini, Hitler ⟶ "Condor Legion" (planes, tanks, technicians)

Surrender of Madrid:
General Franco becomes "caudillo" (leader)

March 30, 1939

2. Stunde: The Opening Situation / The Officer

Unterrichtsschritte	Unterrichtsformen	Fragestellungen
1. Unterrichtsschritt: Textvortrag	Band (oder Lehrer; oder vorbereiteter Schülervortrag)	– You've read Hemingway's "Old Man at the Bridge"; let's hear it again before we talk about it.
2. Unterrichtsschritt: Kurzer Vergleich von Kriegsbericht und Kurzgeschichte	Unterrichtsgespräch	– What do you consider the basic difference between Hemingway's war report "The Bombing of Tortosa" and his short story "Old Man at the Bridge"? (With regard to content? With regard to form?)
3. Unterrichtsschritt: The Opening Situation of "Old Man at the Bridge"	Fragend-entwickelndes Verfahren ——► T 2 ——► T 3	– What situation is described at the opening of this short story? – Can we draw a rough sketch of the situation? (——► T 2) – On what side of the bridge is the old man sitting? – Do we know why the old man is sitting by the side of the road? – Where in the beginning of the text is the first suggestion of a war situation? What other hints make this clearer? – What contrast exists between the old man and the people around him? (——► T 3)
4. Unterrichtsschritt: The Officer	Unterrichtsgespräch ——► T 4	– Who describes the situation? – Why has the narrator come to the bridge? – What do we learn about the type of person the narrator is from the way he presents himself? (——► T 4) – How would you characterize the conversation that is going on between the officer and the old man? – What do you make of the way the officer keeps watching the far end of the bridge? – What effect does the repeated mention of the carts have on the reader? – Does the officer really understand the old man?

Homework: (falls keine Doppelstunde zur Verfügung steht)

Read the short story again.
Do you think the officer really understands the old man?
Quote from the text to support your arguments.

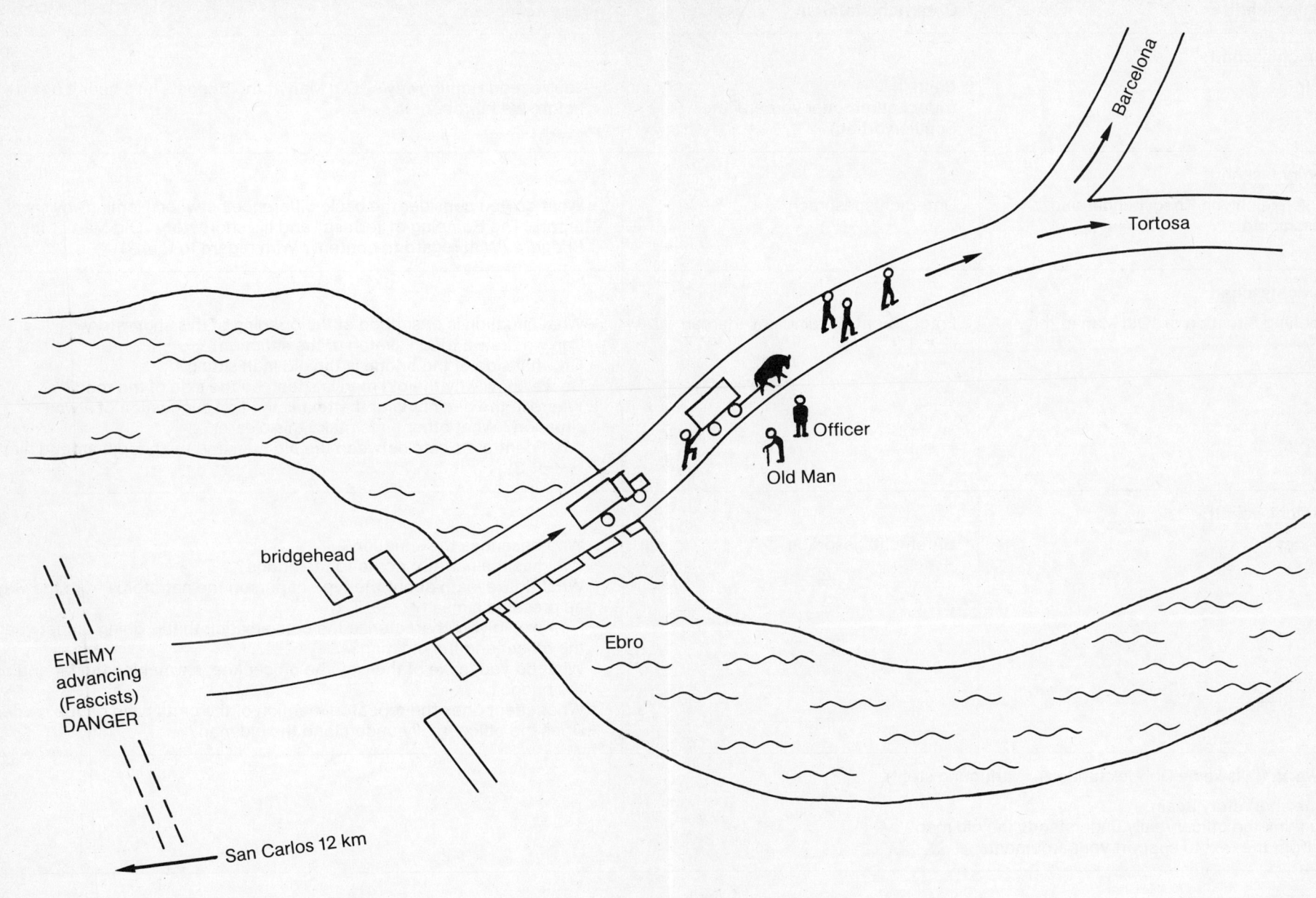

Barcelona

Tortosa

Officer

Old Man

bridgehead

ENEMY
advancing
(Fascists)
DANGER

Ebro

San Carlos 12 km

T3

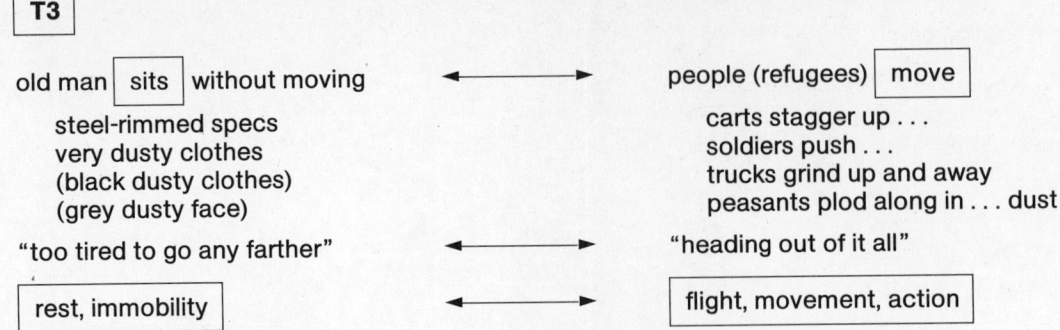

old man | sits | without moving ←——————→ people (refugees) | move

    steel-rimmed specs   carts stagger up . . .
    very dusty clothes   soldiers push . . .
    (black dusty clothes)   trucks grind up and away
    (grey dusty face)   peasants plod along in . . . dust

"too tired to go any farther" ←——————→ "heading out of it all"

| rest, immobility | ←——————→ | flight, movement, action |

T4

The Officer

factual
unemotional   }   " . . . my business to cross the bridge, . . . explore . . ., find out . . ."

friendly
concerned
(but non-committal)   }   talks to the old man, shows an interest in him

observant
watchful   }   watches bridge and bridgehead ("not so many carts now, very few people . . .")
alert

                watches bridge and Ebro Delta country ("wondering how long . . .", "listening all the while . . .", expecting enemy contact)

                watches the far end of bridge (" . . . a few last carts hurrying . . .")

                watches the far bank   (" . . . now no carts")

sympathetic   urges the old man to go: "This is not a good place to stop."

resigned
stoic   }   "There was nothing to do about him."

Nick has got to face a new conflict immediately after he has escaped the one just experienced.

When George is quite certain that the gangsters have crossed the street and disappeared, he goes into the kitchen to untie Sam and Nick. Sam's emphatically repeated "I don't want any more of that" seems to indicate that this is not the first time that the cook has been harshly exposed to brute force. Nick, however, "had never had a towel in his mouth before." The express mention of the towel conveys an unpleasant, suffocating sensation to the reader. For the first time in his life Nick has been physically maltreated. He finds it hard to cope with this experience. "Say, what the hell?" he says, pretending a superiority he does not possess. Inside, surely, Nick must be considerably shaken up. But we can only guess; Hemingway is particularly sparing of words in this passage. The men exchange just a few sentences; there is only a minimum of descriptive text. George tells the other two who the killers had come for. Sam, feeling the corners of his mouth still hurting from the gag, is frightened and inquires if the gangsters have really left the place.

Then George suddenly turns to Nick with the suggestion "You better go see Ole Andreson." Nick, who up to this point in the story has been very much on the periphery of the action, who was an observer at the beginning and was then tied up out of sight in the kitchen, is now called upon to abandon his passive role and to act. He responds with an automatic "All right". But the cook interferes loudly and warns Nick with great emphasis to "stay way out of it". "You better not have anything to do with it at all." Thus Nick unexpectedly finds himself between two completely contrary positions: George recommends seeing Ole Andreson (i. e. informing Ole, warning him of the danger he is in), Sam strictly advises against this and tells Nick to keep out of it.

What attitudes do George and the cook represent respectively? To answer this question it may be helpful to consider how George and Sam have behaved so far in the story. George has kept his head throughout; he tried to cope with the situation as best he could under the circumstances. He prudently swallowed all the abuse and insults of the gangsters, and "played along". Now, again, he acts pragmatically, suggesting that someone should go and warn Ole Andreson. But why doesn't he go himself? Is it because he can't leave the lunch-room, or is he afraid of possible consequences? Is he genuinely concerned about Ole, out of a sense of responsibility, or is his concern only skin-deep? "Don't go if you don't want to." he says to Nick and leaves the seriousness of the matter undiscussed. Nick must choose. Should he follow the cook's advice and "stay out of it"? But the cook has shown himself to be a coward, a man who would rather submit to brute force than risk being hurt. Or should Nick follow George's suggestion and try to save Ole's life? His choice is between involvement or evasion. Nick's decision is made quickly: "I'll go see him." He is determined not to let the unscrupulous gangsters commit their crime; he has experienced some of their brutality and feels it his duty to thwart them if he can.

When Nick has made his choice and has made the decision to go and see Ole Andreson, the cook turns away. "Little boys always know what they want to do." He realizes the danger involved in Nick's decision to help. Nick is about to risk his own life in order to save Ole's. Intermingled with the cook's concern and bitterness is a hint at Nick's youthfulness. Entirely unmoved by the cook's comments, George then tells Nick where he can find Ole.

Only when the short story has been read to the end will it become clear that this scene has the quality of a real tragedy to it: a human being is confronted with a supposed freedom of choice. "Ti draso?", "How shall I act?" is the unanswered question in Greek tragedy, where invariably human action leads ultimately to suffering and despair because a "right" choice does not exist for humans in situations where there is no way out. The discussion of this brief central passage reveals the importance of Nick as the actual protagonist of this short story. Although not apparent at first it becomes increasingly clearer that Hemingway's main interest is focused on Nick. Nick is the only character present in every one of the five "scenes" of the story.

Unterrichtsschritt 4:
Possible Consequences of Nick's Decision?

Provided that the students have not read the end of the story yet they could be invited to discuss how they think the story will continue. How do they visualize Nick's encounter with Ole? What result do they expect from Nick's visit to Ole? Their speculations could be interesting and stimulating. Quite likely they may be thinking of some dramatic culmination, perhaps a shoot-out, with someone (Ole? the gangsters?) getting killed. Movie clichés may be re-hashed. (*Alternative:* the students could be asked to write an ending of their own, as homework, before reading on.)
The point in inviting the students' speculations is to make them sensitive to the fact that Hemingway, contrary to cliché gangster stories and films, does not make use of any of the stereotype devices at all, as will be seen.

Hausaufgabe:

Auf dem Hintergrund der Spekulationen und Erwartungen der Schüler hinsichtlich eines möglichen Endes der Geschichte soll die häusliche Vorbereitung des Schlusses der Short Story an Interesse gewinnen. Was

Nick dann wirklich erlebt, ist ebenso unerwartet wie aufschlußreich. Die Leitfragen: "How is Ole Andreson described?" and "Comment on his behaviour" sollen die Schüleraufmerksamkeit auf recht offensichtliche Diskrepanzen lenken.

6. Stunde:
Nick's Involvement

Unterrichtsschritt 1:
The Outcome of Nick's Efforts

To start with, the students' speculations and suggestions regarding the possible outcome of Nick's mission are contrasted with Hemingway's presentation of Ole Andreson's surprisingly passive attitude.
Then the final part of the text is subdivided into two parts (= homework): from "Outside the arc-light shone . . ." to "Goodnight, the woman said", and from "Nick walked up the dark street . . ." to the end. The headlines to be found could be
a) Nick's Involvement
b) Nick's Lesson
or, more explicitly,
a) Nick's attempt to help Ole Andreson
b) Nick learns a lesson about life.

Unterrichtsschritt 2:
The Atmosphere Outside

Most of the action of this short story takes place inside; there are very few references to the outside, and only two very short passages (Nick's walk to and from Hirsch's rooming-house) where the outside is described, if only in barest outlines. When Nick leaves the lunch-room to find his way to Ole Andreson, Hemingway mentions the arc-lights, the bare branches of a tree, car tracks. What kind of atmosphere is depicted here? Arc-lights produce a cold, glaring light and sharp shadows, the barren branches suggest the coming cold of winter and barrenness, the car tracks in a dusty road suggest the anonymity of cars passing through the town; the overall impression is one of coldness, desolation, unfriendliness. The hostile atmosphere just experienced inside seems to find a correspondence in the atmosphere outside. (→ T 6)

We remember that the street lights are mentioned for the first time at the very beginning of the story, when the two men have entered the room. They are mentioned a second time when the two leave the lunch-room and pass under the arc-light. Now, as Nick leaves, he too passes under this cold light. And again, when he returns from his mission the arc-light is mentioned. Unobtrusively, Hemingway sets meaningful markers, as it were, almost like stage directions.

Unterrichtsschritt 3:
Nick Sees Ole Andreson

The first part of the final passage (from "Outside the arc-light shone..." to "Good-night, the woman said.") is read out by a good student.

Alternative: three students read: from "Outside the arc-light..." to "Come in"; from "Nick opened the door..." to "... looking at the wall"; from "He's been in his room..." to "Goodnight, the woman said".

Ole's room is "at the end of a corridor", a dead end, so to speak, with no means of escape. Maybe the students will notice that the line "Nick opened the door..." recalls the beginning of the short story. ("The door of Henry's lunch-room opened..."); remembering that with the gangsters the threat of murder crossed the threshold at that moment, it is easy to imagine what would have happened if instead of Nick the killers were in the door now! Who, then, is this man Ole Andreson and in what position does Nick find him?

Ole, a former heavyweight prize-fighter, extraordinarily tall ("too long for the bed"), and probably very strong and muscular, is lying in bed (at seven o'clock in the evening!), facing the wall. He doesn't even turn round to look at Nick when the boy enters. As so often with Hemingway we must read between the lines, must infer the implications. How would any normal person react if there was a knock at the door? What does Ole's turning his back towards the person entering indicate? We get the impression that he is acting like a victim who has given up hope and is waiting for the final blow.

Ole's reaction to Nick's excited report about the killers is equally amazing. First he says nothing at all in answer to Nick's "...they were going to kill you." So Nick goes on and repeats the vital piece of information: "They were going to shoot you when you came in..." Can we imagine the disappointment and frustration when, again, there is no response from Ole, who keeps looking at the wall? Nick's third attempt, "George thought I better come and tell you about it.", sounds feeble enough already and shows his helplessness under these unexpected circumstances. At long last Ole says, "There isn't anything I can do about it." What attitude is expressed in these words? This strong man, a boxer, a former prize-fighter, has given up, does not want to fight any more, does not even want to know what the gangsters look like who are after him. The police "wouldn't do any good" either. Nick's desperate question "Isn't there something I could do?" is answered with Ole's hopeless "There ain't anything to do." Not once does Ole look towards Nick who makes several attempts to come up with helpful suggestions. Twice it is mentioned that Ole doesn't look at Nick and six times that he is looking at (talking to, rolling over

45

towards) the wall. Thus Hemingway conjures up the picture of a man in a situation with no way out, a man driven up against the wall, condemned to death, waiting for his execution.

Ole can't "fix it up some way", he "got in wrong" in the boxing business somehow (later on George voices his opinion that the boxer probably "doublecrossed" somebody in Chicago).

Nick, the boy who has come to help, to save human life, is now absolutely helpless as he looks at the big Swede who doesn't even bother to look back at him, but keeps staring apathetically at the wall. Eventually Nick leaves the room and while closing the door takes a last look at the scene in the awareness that his mission has failed.

When Nick has shut the door behind him this marks the end of a scene that both corresponds to and contrasts with the lunch-room scene. The gangsters come prepared to kill and leave without success; Nick goes to Ole prepared to save his life and also leaves without the expected result: these are two inversely related situations that complement each other.

The story could have ended here. But Hemingway adds two short scenes.

Unterrichtsschritt 4:
Confusing Elements in the Story

On his way out Nick gets involved in a conversation with the landlady of the rooming-house who is worried about the Swede's "not feeling well" and who points out to him that Ole is "an awfully nice man", "gentle", and that one wouldn't know he had been in the ring "except from the way his face is" (i. e. it must show signs of having been beaten up in the boxing ring, i. e. a typical boxer's nose, or damaged ears; cf. The Battler!).

How does all this confusing information fit together: heavyweight boxer, strong, but offering no resistance; involved in illegal actions ("double-crossing"), but "awfully nice"; beaten-up boxer's face, but "gentle"? Nick's confusion is heightened further by his mistaking the landlady's identity: she is not Mrs Hirsch, but Mrs Bell!

Why does Hemingway put such irritating elements into the story? What is their effect? Does he want to make his point that appearance and reality are very often two widely differing matters? Where else in the story have we come across similar contradictions? There are quite a few of them: just as Mrs Bell looks after "Hirsch's rooming-house", so George runs "Henry's lunch-room"; the clock that doesn't show the correct time, the lunch-room that used to be a saloon, the paid killers who look "like a vaudeville team" (variety entertainers); the boxer who does not want to fight... (→ T 8)

Nick has got to learn that things are not necessarily what they seem to be. He experiences paradoxes without being able to understand them.

Hausaufgabe:

Die schriftliche Beantwortung der Frage "What is the result of Nick's experience in this story?" wird als Einstieg für die Schlußbesprechung dienen. Zudem sollen die Schüler den Spannungsverlauf der Kurzgeschichte in Form einer Kurve graphisch darzustellen versuchen und eine Begründung für ihre Darstellung geben können.

7. Stunde:
The Result of Nick's Experience

Unterrichtsschritt 1:
The Result of Nick's Experience

Why does Hemingway not have the story end with Nick leaving Mrs Hirsch's rooming-house? Apparently the author intends to stress Nick's reaction to the experience he has just had to undergo. The question "What is the result of Nick's experience?" (= homework) relates to the function of the last "scene" of the short story, and serves as an introduction to the final discussion of "The Killers". A first general answer will make it clear that Hemingway's focal point of interest does not lie with Ole Andreson, but with Nick. The boy's reaction to what he has had to live through this evening, both in the lunch-room and in the hotel, reveals the effect those two experiences have on him: he cannot completely understand, or even rationalize them, but they have left scars on him. Thus, like Ole, Nick is a victim too, if in a different sense.

To bring this out as clearly as possible the end of the story (mostly dialogue again) should be read out with special attention (from "Nick walked up the dark street..." to the end), contrasting Nick's concern and inner involvement with George's seeming indifference and the cook's typical "I-don't-want-to-have-anything-to-do-with-this" attitude ("I don't even listen to it"). The subsequent paraphrase and analysis is to corroborate this further.

After Nick's return to the lunch-room he talks to George about his experience with Ole Andreson; his words show how concerned, helpless and frustrated he is. He speaks in short sentences and there is definitely no attempt to "swagger it off" this time. When George hears that Ole has no intention of running away from danger he takes it for granted that the killers will get

him. It is a foregone conclusion. "They'll kill him." And Nick, too, has got to acknowledge this fact: "I guess they will." Does this mean that Nick accepts brutal reality now? What may his voice sound like when he says these words?

Again he says "I guess so" when George offers his explanation that Ole "must have got mixed up in something in Chicago." And then: "It's an awful thing."

Nick can't stop thinking about the man in his room, condemned to death, waiting till he has picked up enough courage to get up from his bed and to go out, to present himself as a target to his killers, who must be waiting for him out there in the dark somewhere.

For a while there is silence. George busies himself with mechanically wiping the counter. Hopefully by now the students have grasped that the very few descriptive sentences which Hemingway inserts into the dialogue usually contain some significant signal. In this instance it is the unobtrusive reference to the towel. How must Nick feel when he sees George habitually wiping the counter with a towel of the sort he himself had been gagged with only a short while ago? Hemingway makes no comment.

Nick breaks the silence with a question showing that he just cannot stop thinking about Ole, "I wonder what he did?" George immediately knows an answer, a matter-of-fact type of explanation: "Double-crossed somebody. That's what they kill them for." (The students should paraphrase the term "double-crossing". In boxing, and especially in prize-fighting, a lot of money is at stake. This includes betting, too. George believes that Ole had accepted bribes from both sides to manipulate the outcome of a boxing match. The deceived party is now taking revenge, Mafia-style!)

George's sober explanation shows that he is able to rationalize even the atrocity of planned murder. Nothing seems to unbalance him. He appears to be very much back to normal behind his counter. Nick, however, may be remembering Mrs Bell's comment on Ole "He's an awfully nice man, you know . . . He's just as gentle." How does this characterization go with "double-crossing", bribery, foul play, corruption? Nick cannot understand such discrepancies. The idea that just one block of houses away someone is waiting for his murderers, the knowledge that there is nothing he can do about this situation, and the realization that life is going on as usual, as if nothing had happened, weighs so heavily on the boy that he arrives at a sudden decision: he is going to leave the town! When, perhaps unexpectedly, George approves of Nick's decision to leave, the boy explains his reason, "I can't stand thinking about him waiting in the room and knowing he's going to get it. It's too damn awful." George's final sentence, "You better not think about it" is blatantly unrealistic; Nick cannot think of anything else!

Unterrichtsschritt 2:
Nick's Lesson

Nick's intention to turn his back on the town indicates an attempt to run away from a reality which he has come into contact with, but which he, (unlike George) cannot cope with yet. He is running away from the depressing fact that – contrary to the ideas suggested in the movies where the "goodies" always win a victory over the "baddies" in the end – it is not always goodness that keeps the upper hand in this world. He is running away from the realization that human beings are capable of mean, ruthless, unscrupulous actions; from the cowardice of those who don't want to get involved, and the indifference of those who have resigned themselves to this reality; from the phenomenon that so frequently there is an abyss between appearance and reality.

Ultimately, Nick is trying to run away from evil in this world. He is young enough still to cling to the naive hope that the world is better elsewhere. It is not hard to imagine that life holds all sorts of extreme experiences and disappointments in store for him, in the years ahead. ("The Battler", for instance, could be interpreted as the direct continuation of "The Killers": Nick is on his way again, as a hobo, and again encounters situations and human behaviour that he is incapable of comprehending.)

Nick's last name is Adams. Just as Adam, the first man, loses paradise – albeit through his own fault – Nick, too, the young adolescent, loses the paradise of his childhood with its naive faith in appearances and its firm belief in right and wrong. Nick is beginning to realize that the world around him is by no means in a reliable state of order. His experience with the killers forces him to view the world of adults in a new light; he finds himself confronted with aspects of human existence he was not familiar with before, and he is considerably shaken up by this confrontation. The shock of initiation he has received comes out in Nick's decision to leave the town. (Note: The terms "initiation" and "story of initiation" should be explained in this context.)

The adult world of Hemingway's stories is a hard and cruel world. Nick Adams, too, will be an adult one day. How will he act then, at moments when courage and involvement are called for? Will he behave like Sam, or like George, or possibly like Ole Andreson? Or will he decide to act the same way he has done now, as young Nick? Hemingway chose a first name for the boy that is also a name for the devil ("Old Nick"). Is this meant as a hint that the boy, too, will go in a negative direction as he grows older? A tacit understanding that he might eventually get more pragmatic (like George), more submissive (like Sam), more resigned to the evil in this world (like Ole)? Might this young adolescent's name perhaps be understood as a generic name suggesting the "old Adam" in all human beings, and the potential of evil that is inherent in every man?

The teacher must decide whether questions concerning a possible interpretation of the protagonist as an almost archetypal figure, and thoughts concerning Hemingway's view of life, should be followed up with the students, or not. If more Hemingway short stories are to be read, such a discussion should be left to the end of the teaching unit. (cf. Hemingway's View of Life in "The Battler", p. 64)

Unterrichtsschritt 3:
Analyse des Gesamtaufbaus der Kurzgeschichte

Die Schüler hatten die Aufgabe, eine Spannungskurve der Short Story zu entwickeln. Anhand eines von einem Schüler an die Tafel gezeichneten (und dann von den anderen diskutierten und ergänzten) Beispiels wird noch einmal der Gesamtaufbau der Kurzgeschichte rückblickend betrachtet.

Dabei sind auch Hinweise auf typische Strukturmerkmale einer Short Story möglich (wie z. B. *open beginning* und *open ending, episodic plot, limited number of persons,* etc.), obwohl eine genauere Betrachtung der Gattung Short Story einem späteren Stadium vorbehalten bleiben sollte. Es wäre auch möglich, über die „Räume" der Kurzgeschichte zu sprechen und sie mit einer klei-

nen Skizze zu veranschaulichen: der Ungemütlichkeit und Unpersönlichkeit des Lunchrooms entspricht die Anonymität des Hotelzimmers. Zwischen diesen beiden Räumen liegt die mit dem kalten Licht der Bogenlampen erhellte Straße mit den kahlen Bäumen: die Unwirtlichkeit des Außenraums korrespondiert mit den Innenräumen und dem Geschehen, das sich in beiden abspielt.

Weiterführende Fragestellungen

Zum Abschluß der Besprechung dieser Kurzgeschichte könnten sich Untersuchungen der Sprache und des Stils Hemingways in "The Killers" anschließen. (Vgl. dazu: Hemingway's Language and Style in "The Battler", p. 64.) Falls im Anschluß an "The Killers" nicht noch Hemingways "The Battler" als weitere Nick-Adams-Story in der Klasse besprochen werden soll, könnten durch ein Schülerreferat (von einem Schüler oder mehreren Schülern vorbereitet) Inhalt und Problematik dieser Kurzgeschichte vorgetragen werden. In jedem Fall sollten die Schüler zur zusätzlichen Lektüre von "The Battler" angeregt werden.

Im übrigen wäre bereits an dieser Stelle eine interessante Aufgabenstellung denkbar (die im Anschluß an "The Battler" angeregt wird), nämlich die Schüler zu eigenem *creative writing* zu stimulieren.

Aufgabenstellung etwa: "Write your own short story, describing an episode that Nick experiences after leaving the town."

The Battler

Wie es der Titel schon andeutet, gehört Hemingways Kurzgeschichte "The Battler" in die Nähe von "The Killers". Obwohl die beiden Short Stories inhaltlich nicht unmittelbar miteinander korrespondieren, könnte "The Battler" doch geradezu die Fortsetzung von Nicks Erlebnis in Henrys Lunchroom sein. Am Ende der Geschichte "The Killers" beschließt der junge Nick Adams, die Stadt zu verlassen, in der er unfreiwillig Zeuge von menschenverachtender Brutalität geworden ist. Er versucht gleichsam, vor dem Bösen in der Welt davonzulaufen. In der Geschichte "The Battler" befindet sich Nick als Tramp unterwegs, ohne klar definiertes Ziel. (*"He must get to somewhere."*) Und wieder erlebt er zwei gefährliche Situationen, die wie Variationen eines Themas aufeinander bezogen scheinen. Zunächst wird er vom Bremser eines Güterzuges hereingelegt und brutal vom Zug hinuntergeprügelt und landet reichlich zerschunden in einer unwirtlichen, neblig kalten Sumpflandschaft neben den Bahngeleisen. Als er ein Lagerfeuer in einer Waldlichtung sieht, will er sich nicht ein weiteres Mal hereinlegen lassen (*"They would never suck him in that way again."*) und schleicht sich daher erst einmal vorsichtig an das Feuer heran, bevor er in die Lichtung hinaustritt. Er wird dann von zwei Männern, Ad Francis, einem weißen ehemaligen Boxer (vgl. Ole Andreson!) und Bugs, einem Schwarzen, bewirtet; doch die Situation ist alles andere als behaglich und harmlos, wie dem Leser alsbald bewußt wird. Der ehemalige Boxer verhält sich nämlich recht merkwürdig, bezeichnet sich mehrfach stolz als *crazy,* und sein anfänglich friedliches (wenn auch seltsames) Verhalten schlägt während des Essens am Lagerfeuer plötzlich auf bedrohliche Weise

um, wird lauernd aggressiv, bösartig. Die unaufhörlich ansteigende Spannungskurve erreicht ihren Höhe- und zugleich Wendepunkt, als Ad Francis auf Nick losgeht, um ihn niederzuprügeln, im gleichen Augenblick jedoch seinerseits von Bugs mit einem Schlag über den Schädel zu Boden gestreckt wird.

In dem sich anschließenden Gespräch zwischen dem Neger und Nick wird das ambivalente Verhältnis zwischen männlicher Selbstbehauptung im Kampf und dem Hinnehmenmüssen von Niederlagen, zwischen Härte und Schwäche, aber auch zwischen menschlichem Sichfinden und Auseinandergehen, einander Helfen und einander Ausbeuten, Normalität und Verrücktheit, in mehrfacher Brechung angesprochen, ohne daß Nick alles, was er hört, richtig zu begreifen vermag. Verwirrt zieht er nach dieser Begegnung weiter auf ansteigenden Gleisen, die sich irgendwo in den Bergen verlieren und deren Ziel er nicht kennt.

Nicks Erlebnis ist ein weiterer Meilenstein auf seinem Weg ins Erwachsenwerden. Wieder sind ihm die Augen ein Stück weit für menschliche Verhaltensweisen in der Wirklichkeit dieser Welt geöffnet worden. "The Battler" gehört somit ebenfalls in den Kreis der sogenannten *stories of initiation*.

Zum methodischen Vorgehen

Hemingways "The Battler" besteht aus drei Teilen von unterschiedlicher Länge: einer zwar nur eineinhalb Seiten langen, aber inhaltlich sehr dichten Exposition, die rückblickend auch die Vorgeschichte mit einbezieht (*Nick has been knocked off the freight-train and is now hiking along the track*); dem Hauptteil (*Nick leaves the track and expe-*

Übersicht über die Unterrichtseinheit „The Battler"

Stunde	Zentrales Stundenthema	Text	Stundeninhalt
1+2	I a) Nick Busted Off the Freight Train I b) Hiking Along the Track	From the beginning to …nearly to Mancelona. from: Three or four miles of swamp. to: …walked into the fire-light.	Background information. Leads up to the short story "The Battler". Discussion of the setting. Description of Nick. Analysis of his situation. The atmosphere.
3	II Nick and the Man by the Fire	from: The man sat there… to: … "She never speeds up."	Nick's strange encounter with a crazy former boxer, and his embarrassed reaction.
4	III a) Nick Adams, Ad Francis and Bugs III b) The Bread Episode	from: A man dropped down… to: …dropped the blackjack on the grass.	The effect of the Negro's arrival on Nick. Gradual build-up of tension. The former prize-fighter's sudden mad attack on Nick.
5	IV Talking About the Former Prize-Fighter	from: The little man lay there… to: …looked childish in repose.	Confusing paradoxes of human behaviour
6	V Nick Moves On	from: "I can wake him" …to the end.	Discussion of the meaning of the end of the story, and of the story as a whole. The result of Nick's experience. Hemingway's language and style in "The Battler".

riences the episode at the fire); und einem knappen Schlußabschnitt (*Nick returns to the track and hikes on*).

Um die Schüler zu einem besseren Verständnis der Kurzgeschichte zu bringen, bietet es sich an, "The Battler" in zwei Abschnitten lesen und vorbereiten zu lassen; zunächst den Anfang bis „Nick stepped out and walked into the firelight.", und später, zur 3. Stunde, den Rest der Geschichte. Auf diese Weise wird die Short Story in zwei sinnvollen, in sich aufeinander bezogenen Ganzheiten gelesen. Alternative dazu wäre: Lektüre in drei Schritten; nach dem Expositionsteil lesen die Schüler zur 3. Stunde zunächst nur

bis "…. 'She never speeds up.'", dann zur 4. Stunde den Rest.

Darüber hinaus werden dann, schrittweise vorgehend, kleinere Teilabschnitte mit Hilfe von Leitfragen genauer analysiert.

Die Planung dieser Unterrichtseinheit ist mindestens auf 6 Stunden angelegt. Um Zeitdruck zu vermeiden, wäre es jedoch wünschenswert, wenn für die 4. und 6. Stunde jeweils eine Doppelstunde zur Verfügung stünde. In Klasse 11 mit nur drei Wochenstunden Englisch steht oft eine Doppelstunde im Wechsel mit einer Einzelstunde zur Verfügung. "The Battler" ließe sich vorzüglich in dieser Abfolge besprechen. In 5 Sitzungen, beginnend und endend mit einer Doppelstunde, könte die Kurzgeschichte in angemessen genauer Betrachtung besprochen werden.

Aufgabe zur 1. Stunde

Die Schüler lesen den Anfang (I a + b) bis "... walked into the firelight" und bereiten den Abschnitt sprachlich vor.

1. Stunde:
Nick Busted off the Freight Train

Unterrichtsschritt 1:
Hinführung zur Short Story "The Battler"

Die Schüler haben den Anfang der Kurzgeschichte bis "... and walked into the firelight" zu Hause vorbereitet, wissen also, daß es in dieser Geschichte um einen Jungen geht, der als Tramp auf einem Zug erwischt und hinuntergeprügelt wird, und irgendwo in der Weite des Landes einen Bahndamm entlangmarschiert.

Als kurze Hinführung zu diesem Thema bieten sich mehrere Möglichkeiten. Es könnte (möglicherweise unter Hinzuziehung einiger Dias oder Photos) die Weite der amerikanischen Landschaft in Erinnerung gerufen werden, die oft über viele Meilen nur von den geraden, schier endlosen Straßen und Geleisen der Züge, welche vornehmlich für den Güterverkehr die Städte miteinander verbinden, durchzogen wird. Die Bedeutung dieser Zugstrecken war vor fünfzig oder hundert Jahren noch weitaus größer als heute, und das Trampen auf Güterzügen stellte eine beliebte Fortbewegungsmöglichkeit dar, wie aus Abenteuerfilmen wohlbekannt ist. Vielleicht könnte in Anknüpfung an bekannte Filme über die Gefahren, denen Tramps früher ausgesetzt waren, anschaulich berichtet werden. So gab es höchst drasti-

sche Methoden, die von einigen Bremsern (*brakemen*) angewendet wurden, um ungebetene Mitfahrer auf den Zügen loszuwerden. Wenn sie etwa Tramps im Gestänge unter den Waggons vermuteten, ließen sie zuweilen eine Eisenstange an einem langen Seil unter den Wagen auf den Schwellen aufschlagen; diese „tanzte" dann auf und ab und verletzte die versteckten Mitreisenden oft lebensgefährlich.

Eine andere Möglichkeit der Hinführung zum Thema wäre die Frage, warum überhaupt früher junge Menschen als Tramps durch die Staaten gezogen sind, was für Ziele und Hoffnungen sie wohl haben mochten. Der Bezug zu heutigen „Aussteigern" wäre möglich, der Vergleich mit *runaway kids* in den USA bietet sich an; die Parallele zum *hitchhiking* unserer Tage würde die Unterschiede zu früheren Zeiten deutlich werden lassen.

Da diese Hinführung zum Thema nur als Einstieg in die Short Story gemeint ist, sollte damit nicht viel Zeit verloren werden. Sie könnte, je nach Unterrichtszusammenhang, auch entfallen.

Unterrichtsschritt 2:
Textpräsentation des Anfangs

Unter der Voraussetzung, daß der Anfang der Geschichte bis "... walked into the firelight." von den Schülern präpariert worden ist, liest ein guter Schüler den ersten Teil bis "... nearly to Mancolona." vor.

Der Lehrer gibt den Schülern Gelegenheit, nach eventuell unverstanden gebliebenen Wörtern zu fragen und überprüft seinerseits gezielt das Verständnis einiger Vokabeln (z. B.: track, swamp, brakeman, bump, embankment, rails). Zur Überprüfung des Globalverständnisses wird eine kurze Paraphrase verlangt, ohne zunächst auf Einzelheiten einzugehen. Sollten die Schüler jedoch bereits Detailbeobachtungen miteinfließen lassen, könnten diese für den Tafelanschrieb verwertet werden. Der Schwerpunkt der Besprechung im folgenden Unterrichtsschritt liegt zunächst auf der *setting;* daran anschließend soll Nick genauer beschrieben werden.

Unterrichtsschritt 3:
Nick Busted Off the Freight Train

"Nick stood up. He was all right." – The story begins right in the middle of a movement, like a film clip arbitrarily cut out of the middle of a scene. The focus is on Nick. He is referred to at the very opening of the story and again at the beginning of each of the following sentences. Although the importance of the central character is thus stressed from the start we don't receive any further information as to who Nick is, how old he is, or where he comes from. Nick has just been knocked off the freight train that is steaming out of sight up the track, and looks around him. Where is he? He is standing by the side of the railroad track, and as darkness falls he can make out water on both sides of the track, and swamp. The track is elevated, on an embankment, and "like a causeway (goes) on ahead through the swamp". To get to the water Nick must go down the slope of the embankment.

What can we say about the setting then? It is dark, and Nick is "a long way off from anywhere." Alone in the dark, surrounded by water and swamp, miles away from the nearest town – this suggests a feeling of gloom and isolation; nature seems hostile and dangerous. Nick knows that he must not stay here long, he "must get to somewhere". So he follows the track that is compared to a causeway through the swamp, suggesting firmness, "solid walking", direction, movement toward a goal. However, we don't know if Nick has any definite goal, any specific destination. The names of two towns that he has passed and of the next town en route are mentioned, but remain without any closer geographical definition, they don't play any part in the story. The railroad track that is mentioned so often and that basically constitutes the setting at the beginning of the story, assumes a symbolic significance from the start. The track that emanates from somewhere and goes to places unknown seems symbolic of Nick's journey through this particular phase of his life, which is characterized by his fluctuating between security and insecurity, "solid walking" on a "smooth roadbed", and being knocked off a running train by some brutal brakeman.

(Unless noticed by the students, a discussion of the significance of the railroad track should be left until the end of the story.)

After the analysis of the setting at the opening of the short story the students should infer the information that we get about Nick. Although not badly hurt when falling off the train, he has scraped his hands and knee, his hands are dirty, his pants torn. Also he is adorned with a black eye and a swelling over his eye.

While bathing his knee in the cold water below the embankment his thoughts return to "that lousy crut of a brakeman" and the way he had tricked Nick's confidence. Nick is furious and thinks of revenge; however, he is at least as angry with himself as he is mad at the brakeman. The brakeman had "sucked" him, and he had "fallen for it", like a naive, trusting kid. The word kid is mentioned three times in this flashback. Whereas "kid" in normal parlance can mean about the same as "youngster", just implying that the person is still relatively young, Nick now interprets the word as meaning child-like, childish, immature, as with great annoyance he blames himself for the "lousy kid thing" that he has done.

The fact that Nick remembers this scene and relives it mentally, could make the teacher draw his students' attention to the so-called "flashback" technique. The term "flashback" might be explained in passing; a brief comparison with corresponding film-techniques will suffice. (Cf. Arbeitsblatt Literary Terms, p. 79.)

But Nick has learnt a lesson from his experience: he won't be tricked so easily again! From now on he is going to be more careful. He won't act like a kid again!

Hausaufgabe:

Falls keine Doppelstunde zur Verfügung steht, müßte die Besprechung mit der Beschreibung Nicks abbrechen. Die Schüler lesen den Anfang noch einmal ganz durch und achten diesmal besonders darauf, welche Wörter auffallend häufig verwendet werden. Außerdem sollen sie versuchen, die beschriebene *setting* mit ein paar Strichen als Situationsskizze aufzuzeichnen.

2. Stunde:
Hiking Along the Track

Unterrichtsschritt 1:
Wiederholung der Ergebnisse

Für den Fall, daß keine Doppelstunde zur Verfügung steht, würde die zweite Stunde mit einer kurzen Rekapitulation des bereits besprochenen Inhalts beginnen. Sodann würden Schüler den Anfang der Short Story bis "... walked into the fire-light." noch einmal vorlesen, wobei dieses Mal der Vortrag der Schüler bereits ein wenig in Richtung auf „interpretierendes Lesen" gehen sollte, da der Anfangsteil nun mehrfach durchgegangen worden ist. Wenn das in der ersten Stunde erarbeitete Tafelbild auf einer Folie festgehalten wurde, so kann der sich nunmehr anschließende Anschrieb das Tafelbild T 1 beziehungsvoll ergänzen.

Unterrichtsschritt 2:
Nick Hiking Along the Track

After Nick has recovered from the shock, washed his hands and bathed his wounds, he starts up the track and walks along with regular strides trying to put his feet on the ballast between the ties. So he hikes along "putting the miles of track behind him." How is this hiking described by Hemingway? It is a strenuous affair for Nick. The swelling over his eye hurts, he is hungry, he must watch where he steps. And then there is the constant presence of the swamp, "ghostly in the rising mist", – unpleasant, eerie, dangerous. Maybe the students will have noticed how often the words "track" and "swamp" are used in the opening part. (The word "track" appears 13 times, the word "swamp" five times; darkness is mentioned 4 times). Why does Hemingway repeat these words so often, especially the word "track"? Obviously, the repetition of the words shows their importance, both for Nick and for the reader. Nick's mind is occupied first and foremost with this track which he must follow if he wants to get out of the unfriendly hostile setting, and he is still young enough to have his imagination affected by the mist on the swamp that rises in all sorts of "ghostly" shapes and probably frightens him. To the reader however, the insistence on those words makes them assume a greater significance, almost a symbolic meaning. (This becomes clearer at the very end of the story, so a discussion of the symbolic implications could be left until the end.)

When Nick comes up to and then crosses an iron bridge, "his boots ringing hollow on the iron", the sense of danger is intensified. Suddenly there is no solid ballast between the ties any more, instead he can see the water down below, showing black between the slits of the ties. He kicks a loose spike and it drops down into the cold black water.

What if Nick tripped and fell through himself, like the loose spike?

Then, off to one side of the track, where the country opens out after a clearing in the forest, Nick notices a fire. A fire in the wilderness of this swamp landscape, a light in the darkness – what a relief. A fire normally signals warmth and security. But the way Nick responds when he notices the light shows that he has in fact learnt from experience. He moves much more carefully now, creeps up the track a little further, and then down the embankment. (The word "carefully" is repeated!) Sneaking into the forest, he avoids making any noise, is aware of the fallen beechnut burrs under his shoes (cf. the loose spike on the bridge), and quietly comes up to the fire from behind. Before stepping out into the firelight he watches the solitary man who is sitting there looking into the fire.

To ensure a better understanding of the layout of the situation a brief sketch should now be drawn with the help of the students, illustrating the course of the track, the bridge, water, swamp, forest, clearing, fire. (→ T 3)

If there are some minutes left it would be interesting to ask the students what they think will happen when Nick suddenly steps forward from out of the dark towards the man by the fire. This question could stimulate a lively and imaginative discussion provided the students have not already read the rest of the story.

Hausaufgabe:

Entweder lesen die Schüler nun den ganzen Rest der Kurzgeschichte im Zusammenhang, wobei der Abschnitt bis "She never speeds up." sprachlich genau vorbereitet werden müßte, oder aber die Schüler lesen zunächst nur den Abschnitt bis "She never speeds up." und den Rest der Kurzgeschichte erst zur 4. Stunde. Letzteres Verfahren

empfiehlt sich bei Klassen, die im extensiven Lesen noch nicht geübt sind. – Wieder sollen die Schüler besonders auf Schlüsselwörter achten.

3. Stunde:
Nick and the Man by the Fire

Unterrichtsschritt 1:
Textpräsentation

Neben dem obligatorischen Anknüpfen an das in der vorangegangenen Stunde Erarbeitete sollte der Lehrer sich durch eine knappe Vokabelüberprüfung vergewissern, ob die Schüler den aufgegebenen Textabschnitt gewissenhaft präpariert haben. Sodann wird der in sich geschlossene Textabschnitt "The man sat there..." bis "She never speeds up." möglichst lebendig von einem Schüler vorgelesen. (Alternative: zwei Schüler übernehmen die Rollen von Nick und Ad und tragen einen echten Dialog vor. Ein weiterer Schüler liest die wenigen Brückentexte, wobei kurze Einschübe wie *Ad said, Nick said* einfach überlesen werden. – Diese Art des Textvortrags paßt auch gut an das Ende der Stunde; nachdem die Passage besprochen worden ist, können die Schüler mit noch größerem Verständnis schauspielernd lesen.)

Unterrichtsschritt 2:
Nick and the Man by the Fire

How do we expect a man to react who sits looking at a fire in the middle of nowhere when all of a sudden a person steps up to him from out of the dark? Naturally he would be startled, would jump up, show some sort of surprised reaction, possibly be angry. But the man by the fire does not even move when Nick has come quite close to him. Nick's "hello" is left unanswered. Instead, the man looking up at Nick is instantaneously interested in Nick's black eye. When he hears who gave Nick the "shiner" the man is in the picture; he has seen "the bastard" who "busted" Nick (note the phonetic similarity between "bastard" and "busted"). Nick echoes the man's swearword wholeheartedly: "The bastard!" But then, surprisingly, the man comments quite seriously, "It must have made him feel good to bust you." What is Nick to make of that statement? Nick escapes into a some-what childish outburst indicating his thirst for revenge: "I'll bust *him*." (Just as at the beginning of the story he swears that he "would get him some day.") Again, the man's reaction to Nick's posture of revenge is unusual, in fact it is quite horrific, advising Nick as he does to get the brakeman "with a rock some time when he's going through." What is the man really suggesting here? Nick is to lie in ambush and, given the opportunity, is to knock the brakeman off the train with a rock, committing cold-blooded murder?! How does Nick respond to this advice? "I'll get him," he says. This sounds affirmative, yet at the same time elusive. And when the strange man by the fire mistakenly jumps to the conclusion that Nick is a "tough one" and Nick, in response, ventures an honest "No" and is rebuked with "All you kids are tough", his answer shows a certain elusiveness again, obliging with a generalizing "You got to be tough." He gives way to the man's opinion that sets such priority on toughness, and the man is satisfied: "That's what I said."

What then, is the reader's first impression of this lonely man by the fire? Surely his reactions are not "normal" by any standards, and we can imagine Nick's irritation under the circumstances. Nick senses the man's erratic behaviour and doesn't quite know how to act. It is now that Nick has a closer look at the man, at his misshapen, mutilated

face, the sunken nose, queer lips, the eyes that look like slits. A "dead looking" face. To top it all the man has only one ear. The sight of so much ugliness makes Nick a little sick.

But matters get worse when the man tells him with a good amount of self-admiration that he "could take it". "Don't you think I could take it, kid?" he asks, and Nick doesn't seem to take offence from the word "kid". "You bet" is his obligingly admiring answer, clearly not wanting to disagree with the man who goes on to tell Nick how "they all bust their hands" on him and couldn't hurt him.

The students will notice that the man uses the word "bust" again here. What effect is this bound to have on Nick who was "busted" by that "bastard", the brakeman? The man brags that nobody was able to hurt him, whilst Nick has just been badly hurt and can still feel the pain in his face. Moreover, doesn't the man's appearance, his beaten up face and his "cauliflower" ear belie his own words? And strangely, this braggart is just a "little man", as it turns out. Obviously, Nick is very ill-at-ease in this situation and wants to back out as quickly as possible. So although he feels very hungry he doesn't accept the man's offer of some-thing to eat. But now he is hooked. The man doesn't let go of him. With a demanding, domineering "Listen..." he repeatedly addresses Nick and showers a load of unasked-for information on Nick. The greatest effect comes from his simple "I'm not quite right.", "I'm crazy." Nick's immediate impulse – laughter – reveals the boy's uneasiness and nervousness. He pre-tends not to believe the man who then, seriously, repeats his statement, and just as seriously asks Nick if he has ever been crazy. Nick's subsequent question "How does it get you?", conversational though it sounds, barely covers up the boy's uneasiness and perhaps an anticipation of some sudden attack of craziness that might seize the little man.

The man now identifies himself as Ad Francis, a former boxing champion (and a prize fighter, as we'll learn on the next page). He tells Nick the reason why he "beat them"; his heartbeat is much slower than normal. Relentlessly he forces Nick to confirm the truth of his claim. With a battery of imperatives he makes Nick count the pulse of his wrist "Feel it... Come on. Take hold... Put your fingers... Listen. Take hold again..." Nick does as he is told, if hesitatingly, and probably with rather mixed feelings. He obliges, whether counting or not, with the expected answer, and in the end, the little man is satisfied and says happily, referring to his heart, "She never speeds up."

Looking back over this passage the question can now be answered, which words are particularly prominent in it, so that they might be considered keywords. These are the words: bust, beat, tough, take it, crazy. (Written down in this order they reveal a development which shows "craziness" as the ultimate result of taking too many beatings.) It may suffice at this point to note these keywords down on the board and to revert to them at a later stage in the discussion of this short story.

Unterrichtsschritt 3:
Dialogischer Vortrag der Textstelle

Wenn noch genügend Zeit zur Verfügung steht, könnte zum Abschluß der Besprechung dieser Passage die Textstelle von zwei Schülern im Dialog vorgetragen werden, sofern dies nicht bereits zu Beginn der Stunde in dieser Weise erfolgt ist (vgl. oben).

Hausaufgabe:

Die Aufgabenstellung richtet sich nach der Aufgabe zur vorigen Stunde (vgl. S. 55). In jedem Fall sollen die Schüler nunmehr den ganzen Rest der Geschichte lesen und den Abschnitt bis "... blackjack on the grass." sprachlich vorbereiten. Die mitgegebene Leitfrage soll die Schüleraufmerksamkeit vor allem auf Nicks Reaktionen lenken. Die Aufforderung, eine Spannungskurve der Episode am Lagerfeuer nachzuzeichnen zu versuchen, soll den Schülern den dramatischen Aufbau der Szene bewußt machen.

4. Stunde:
Nick Adams, Ad Francis, and Bugs / The Bread Episode

Unterrichtsschritt 1:
Textpräsentation

Mit einer kurzen inhaltlichen Wiederholung der Begegnung Nicks mit Ad Francis wird an die vorangegangene Stunde angeknüpft. Sodann wird der in der folgenden Doppelstunde im Mittelpunkt stehende Textteil "A man dropped down..." bis "... blackjack on the grass." von einem oder mehreren Schülern möglichst überzeugend vorgetragen. (Es empfiehlt sich wieder, drei Schüler die Rollen von Ad, Bugs und Nick übernehmen zu lassen; ein vierter liest die verbindenden Texte.)

Unterrichtsschritt 2:
The Arrival of Bugs

Quite unexpectedly for Nick, a third man appears. Where he has come from and whether he has watched Nick and Ad for some time before dropping down from the embankment is not narrated. What sort of person is he? His name is Bugs, and Nick knows even before seeing him clearly that he is a Negro. Ad introduces him as his "pal" (friend, companion) and adds, "He's crazy, too." Again, we don't know if this is a serious statement or just a joke. The negro's behaviour stands in marked contrast to Ad's blunt and erratic comments; his manner of speaking is extremely polite, unusual under the circumstances. He uses phrases like "glad to meet you", calls the boy "Mr Adams" and refers to him as "the gentleman" (cf. Ad's calling him "kid"!). At the same time there is something very clever and glib about him. He immediately inquires where Nick comes from and his name, but in an indirect way, "Where (did) you say you're from?" as though Nick had already mentioned it, and "I didn't catch your name.", again as though Nick had already said his name. His suave politeness is not consistent though; Ad's unmotivated interjection, for instance, "He says he's never been crazy" is taken up by Bugs with unexpected seriousness, "He's got a lot coming to him." And Bugs' cool comment "I hear most of what goes on" has quite a different ring (and is immediately rebuked by Ad's threatening "That ain't what I asked you"), but is covered up right away by Bugs' obliging answer.

What effect does Bugs' arrival on the scene have on Nick, then? A great deal of the irritation and uneasiness that he must have felt before disappears now that Bugs moves about so normally and acts so efficiently. He now admits his hunger when Ad asks him, whilst before he didn't want to stay and eat with Ad. Nick is, in fact, "hungry as hell", and he relaxes, thoroughly enjoying his tasty ham-and-eggs sandwich. Like a big boy he enthusiastically appreciates having his bread dipped in the ham fat. The situation seems to have changed to Nick's advantage, seems to be sociable, harmless, friendly, amicable. But there are undertones which we must pay attention to.

The episode following Bugs' arrival is a dramatically constructed scene in itself, with an exposition (Bugs' cooking preparations), a central part (containing a gradual build-up of tension due to Ad's strange behaviour), and a climax (Ad's attack on Nick).

The dramatic curve begins to rise when Bugs, who is busy over the fire, frying the ham and breaking eggs into the skillet, politely asks Nick to cut some bread. While Nick is cutting six slices off the loaf he is being watched by Ad, who suddenly leans forward and asks Nick to let him have his knife. At this point, very determined, the Negro interferes. "No, you don't. Hang on to your knife, Mister Adams." These words are strikingly adamant and authoritarian for the otherwise so polite Negro. The former prize-fighter sits back. The seemingly harmless small-talk about the food continues. Then the delicious savoury sandwiches are ready to be served. Mister Francis gets the first sandwich, and after that Nick gets his. Bugs sits down next to Ad, opposite Nick. Ad hasn't participated in the talk about the food. When he gets his sandwich he lets the egg run and Bugs points this out to him. Obviously he is not concentrating on his sandwich, his mind seems to be somewhere else. While Nick is thoroughly enjoying his food the little man sits and eats in ominous silence. "He had said nothing since the Negro had spoken about the knife." In an over-polite manner Bugs offers Nick a slice of bread dipped in the ham fat, which the boy gladly accepts. Ad is looking at Nick. Bugs then, very pointedly, offers some bread to Ad, addressing him with "Mister Adolph Francis", the full name adding intensity and emphasis. But there is no answer from Ad, who just keeps on looking at Nick.

It is apparent now that the seemingly pleasant and sociable atmosphere round the fire has begun to change. There is some tension in the air, undefined as yet, triggered off by the knife, and marked by Ad's strange silence. Bugs' repeated attempts to distract Al fail. His soft, but intense and warning Negro voice is in stark contrast with the strained atmosphere. Ad keeps on looking at Nick, his eyes almost hidden by his cap. By this time Nick has been alerted to the sense of danger that is suddenly in the air. He feels nervous, senses the silence before the storm. Then Ad explodes in a fit of craziness. In a series of furious, mad outbursts, he attacks Nick verbally. His aggressive anger comes out in the wild swearing that he repeatedly puts into his questions. "How the hell do you get..." / "Who the hell do you think...", "Who the hell asked you...", "Where the hell do you think...!" Ad's accusations are, of course, madly distorted, gross exaggerations. Nick never acted "snotty", never smoked Ad's cigars or drank his liquor.

Nick is helpless in the face of this sudden aggressiveness. Like a big child he replies to Ad's question "Who the hell asked you to butt in here?" with an automatic "Nobody". After that Nick just stands there, listening to Ad's irrational accusations and not knowing what to say. Then Ad stands up – a threatening gesture. The verbal aggression is now to be followed by physical aggression. "You yellow-livered (= cowardly!) Chicago bastard. You're going to get your can (= head) knocked off."

Ad uses the swear-word "bastard" again, the word that focused violent aggressive feelings before. Nick is now the focus of Ad's madly aggressive attention, he is the "bastard" to be "busted". And as the boy steps back, the former champion fighter, flat-footed, in boxer fashion, comes after him. In an imperative, provocative manner he challenges Nick to hit him, determined to give Nick "a beating". When it is clear to Ad

that Nick will not be dared into placing the first punch, he prepares to attack. "All right, then, you bastard.", he says and looks down at Nick's feet in concentration for a hammering knock-out blow that is to follow any second now. This is the highest pitch, the moment of greatest tension.

However, the climax of the dramatic curve is, at the same time, its turning point. The relief comes when Bugs surprisingly knocks Ad Francis down from behind with a cloth-wrapped blackjack.

Erarbeitung einer Spannungskurve der Lagerfeuerszene

Der Rest der Stunde dient dazu, den dramatischen Verlauf der Szene am Feuer in Form einer Spannungskurve nachzuverfolgen. Die Schüler sollen ihre eigenen Vorschläge an die Tafel zeichnen und entsprechend erläutern. Die anderen Schüler kommentieren, ändern oder ergänzen die gemachten Vorschläge, so daß schließlich eine vom Gremium akzeptierte Lösung an der Tafel steht (vgl. als Beispiel die Illustration 2, → T 7).

Hausaufgabe:

Sprachlich genaue Vorbereitung des bereits gelesenen Teils "The little man lay there..." bis "... childish in repose." Schriftliche Beantwortung der Frage "What made Ad Francis crazy?"

5. Stunde: Talking About the Former Prize-Fighter

Unterrichtsschritt 1:
Textpräsentation

Als Einstieg in die Stunde wird an die zuletzt besprochene dramatische Szene am Feuer angeknüpft. Sodann fassen Schüler mit eigenen Worten den Inhalt des sich nun anschließenden Gesprächs zwischen Bugs und Nick kurz zusammen und lesen im Anschluß daran den Textabschnitt vor. Es folgt dann die genauere Analyse der Passage, wobei Nicks drei Fragen als Gliederungshilfe dienen können. Die Hausaufgabe der Schüler wird bei der Besprechung der Frage "What made Ad crazy?" abgerufen.

Unterrichtsschritt 2:
Bugs' Behaviour After Knocking Ad out

Ad Francis in his irrational outbreak attempts to knock Nick's head off, but gets tapped "across the base of his skull" himself. Bugs' drastic interference at the right moment indicates that Ad's craziness must, indeed, be considered dangerous. Nick was in real danger for a moment. But now the tension relaxes. The little man is lying face down unconscious and helpless in the grass. Bugs who a minute ago hit Ad hard on the head with a blackjack now puts him down by the fire "gently", splashes some water on his face, "gently" pulls his ears, and places a coat under his head. He obviously knows how to deal with Ad.

Unterrichtsschritt 3:
Talking About Ad

Nick is taken from one extreme to the other. How is he to understand these abrupt changes? One moment he is enjoying his sandwich, the next he finds himself yelled at and attacked, one moment Bugs knocks Ad down, the next he attends to him gently and caringly. Nick's eyes move from the little man in the grass to the blackjack with the flexible whalebone handle, "worn black leather with a handkerchief wrapped around the heavy end." Worn from heavy use, probably, and wrapped so it wouldn't break the little man's skull. Considering this heavy weapon and the visible effect it has had, Bugs' smiling explanation "I didn't want you to hurt him or mark him up no more than he is" sounds somewhat hard to swallow. Is he trying to disguise the fact that Ad is downright dangerous when he has his fit and "gets that way"? Nick seems to sense this when he states, "You hurt him yourself", leaving the question open as to whether or not he could have defended himself against the former boxer.

Bugs claims he knows "how to do it"; he has had to do it so often "to change him" that he has the right feel for it. Bugs knows how much strength is needed to break eggs into the skillet, and he knows how much strength he must put into a tap across Ad's head without breaking his skull. Nick keeps looking at the unconscious little man for a long time, thus unwittingly reversing the roles of the situation that occurred before. However, there is concern in his question when he asks Bugs: "What made him crazy?"

The Negro's answer to his question gives two reasons; a physical reason and a psychological reason. The physical explanation, "He took too many beatings", sounds like an ironical comment on the former prize-fighter's boasting that he "beat them all", and on his threat to Nick "You're going to take a beating." In spite of his slow, regular pump-like heartbeat and in spite of his bulging muscles he was knocked about and beaten up too often and is now obsessed with aggression as a result of his former lifestyle. The second reason for Ad's craziness that Bugs mentions (while leisurely sipping his coffee!) is of a psychological nature. Vague and a bit confusing is Bugs' narration of the circumstances of Ad's strange love affair without a happy ending. It doesn't become clear why the girl Ad married is, at first, considered to be his sister; nor is it clear why Bugs keeps repeating that Ad's wife looked enough like him to be his own twin. A most mysterious affair, confusing in every respect. Before they were married the papers were writing all about "how she loved her brother and how he loved his sister", after their marriage they started having "disagreements" and she left him. Just the same, she sends him money to support him... Does this mean she still cares for him? "He wouldn't be bad-looking without his face all busted." This paradox reminds us of a similar statement on Ole Andreson, the prize-fighter in "The Killers".

Nick's next question "Where did you meet him?" sparks off further explanations, but the way these are offered tends to irritate Nick even more. When Bugs tells Nick that he was in jail "for cutting a man", he says this smilingly, in his customary soft voice! Bugs claims that he liked Ad right away and didn't mind being considered crazy by Ad (sic!), that he enjoys seeing the country and – summing up from his point of view – that he likes "living like a gentleman". The Negro's smooth explanation (note the many "ands"!) contains one paradox after the other; why should he like a mad maniac who was "busting people all the time?" What does he call "seeing the country" if they have to secrete themselves away in a deserted forest near miles of swampland, keeping away from people? What does he consider "living like a gentleman"? Is he actually a bit crazy, too?

The answer to Nick's third question "What do you all do?" cannot clear the confusion in Nick's mind. Bugs and Ad do "nothing. Just

move around." Ad's former manager / sister / wife, a "mighty fine woman" supports them financially.

How is Nick to understand all this confusing information? There are so many contradictions, so many inherent contrasts. Some of these contrasts could be listed, or written on the board, after looking back over the last passage again. (→ T 9)

Hausaufgabe:

Die Schüler sollen die Schlußpassage (ab "I can wake him up...") nochmals lesen und sich vor allem über die letzten drei Zeilen Gedanken machen. Vielleicht fällt ihnen die Symbolhaftigkeit der Situation auf: nach seinem Umweg ist Nick wieder auf den Geleisen, auf denen er weiter marschieren wird (wohin?). Das Feuer in der Lichtung, auf das er zurückblickt, hat jetzt einen ganz anderen Stellenwert als zuvor. Die Frage "What does the track stand for?" könnte zur weiteren Sensibilisierung der Schüler gestellt werden. Die Beantwortung der Frage, aus wie vielen Teilen diese Short Story besteht, dient dem klareren Verständnis des Gesamtaufbaus, der wiederum die Aussage der Geschichte deutlicher verständlich werden läßt.

6. Stunde:
Nick Moves on

Unterrichtsschritt 1:
Kurze Anknüpfung an die vorangegangene Stunde

Wiederum soll nicht mit dem Abrufen der Hausaufgabe begonnen werden (die Beantwortung der Fragen fließt im Laufe der Stunde in den Unterricht mit ein), sondern mit einer knappen Verknüpfung mit dem zuletzt Erarbeiteten. Alsdann kann die Schlußpassage von einem Schüler vorgelesen werden, bevor sie besprochen wird.

Nick Returns to the Track and Moves on

With extreme politeness and suavity Nick is complimented out of the scene of action by the smooth-voiced Negro. "If you don't mind... I don't like to be not hospitable, but... You don't mind, do you... I wish we could ask you to stay the night, but it's just out of the question." In view of the actual situation his manner appears overbearing and slightly insincere. Before Nick has a chance to say anything he finds himself walking away from the fire, across the clearing to the railway tracks. Out of the range of the fire Nick stops to listen. (cf. this with his approach to the fire!) He can hear the little man's voice like a child's complaining of an awful headache, and the soothing Negro comforting him, almost like a nurse.

The last paragraph rounds off Nick's strange encounter at the fire. He climbs the embankment to regain the track that will provide "solid walking" for him again. With what kind of feeling may Nick be looking back at the firelight in the clearing? Once again he has narrowly escaped a dangerous situation. When the brakeman knocked him off the freight train, he got away with a black eye and a bump on his head. No broken bones; "cheap at the price", as Nick decided then. This time, too, he gets away without any physical harm done to him. He even finds he has a ham sandwich in his hand and puts it in his pocket. It will remind him of the experience by the fire when he eats it later on.

Unterrichtsschritt 3:
The Construction of the Short Story

Before discussing the importance of Nick's experience with the "battler", it may be useful to look back at the construction of this short story.

The story consists of three, or, more precisely, of four parts: it begins and ends on the railroad tracks. The first part, in retrospect ("flashback") is the freight train episode when Nick is knocked off the moving train and lands by the side of the track, bruised and hurt. The second part describes Nick's hiking along the embankment until he sees the fire and leaves the track for a detour through the forest.

The third and main part contains Nick's encounter with the battler and his Negro companion, culminating in the bread episode. The fourth and last part completes Nick's detour by taking him back to the track again on which he will continue hiking. The track that Nick is moving on clearly assumes a deeper significance, almost a symbolic meaning. This may have been obvious to attentive students much earlier, but could be discussed now.

Unterrichtsschritt 4:
The Meaning of Hemingway's Short Story "The Battler"

The Meaning of the Setting. The track symbolizes the course of Nick's life at this stage of his development. In this story Nick, who is still a relatively young boy, not even an adolescent, is yet "a long way off from anywhere". His courageous marching along the track should not disguise the fact that he is aware of the dangerous swamp around him, of the uncanny, fearful atmosphere, of the slits between the ties of the bridge, and the cold, dark water below. His path has its pitfalls, and Nick is alone, but he is determined "to get somewhere". The fire in the woods that signals a deceptive security lures him off his track like a will-o-the-wisp, he strays from his path, but after his upsetting experience with the battler, he resumes his journey. Obviously, his life tracks have no definite destination as yet, but the track before him is on a "mounting grade" that leads into hills unknown. Life is going to be an uphill struggle for Nick; he will probably leave the swampland behind, and instead will have to face mountains, and probably new detours, and other unexpected encounters.

The Meaning of Nick's Journey. In this connection the question of the reason for Nick's journeyings might be raised. Why is Nick a tramp? If the students have read "The Killers" they will assume that Nick is running away from instances of human behaviour that he cannot understand yet and doesn't want to accept. What does Nick expect to find on his journey? Does he expect examples, perhaps, of values worth living for, of more humane life styles, of more optimistic, positive aspects of life? If so, what can we say about the reality that Nick is confronted with in this short story? The violence of the brakeman, the aggressive craziness of the "battler", the paradoxically "gentle" brutality of the Negro? What kind of lifestyles are these? In a final summing up of the characters Ad and Bugs, the ambiguous symbiosis of the two men should be analysed, and the relevance of their existence to Nick's. (→ T 10) It will be seen that there are some striking parallels between Nick and Ad Francis. Outwardly, Nick's bruised body, his black eye and the bump on his forehead correspond to Ad's mutilated, misshapen face. Nick is on the move as a tramp, so are Ad and his companion. Nick however is young, almost a child, whilst Ad is an adult (whose face yet "looks childish in repose"). Nick has just been beaten by the brakeman, Ad has had many, too many, beatings in his life. – Ad and Bugs have come to the end of the road; they keep away from society, – a society that was instrumental in making them the way they are now. Nick however, has only just started on his road, is still searching, if already bruised. Nick is only "scraped", not permanently hurt. This is essential.

From his contact with the brakeman he has learnt to be less trusting on his journey, to be more careful in future. Will he learn something from Ad's beaten-up existence as well? Does he realize that the answer "You got to be tough" is *not* valid in the end? Or will he eventually end up just like Ad, without a home, alone, accompanied by a parasite, doing nothing? We remember Bugs' serious comment "He's got a lot coming to him" referring to Nick's never having been crazy. We may also remember the Negro saying that Ad took "such a liking" to Nick; does this perhaps mean that Ad saw in Nick a "tough one" who was going to be like him one day, a battler?
There is also a strange connection between Nick and Ad through their names: they have part of their names in common, Nick *Ad*ams and *Ad* Francis. It looks as if the name "Ad" might indicate a mutilated Adam. And that reminds us of the first Adam who lost paradise through his own fault (cf. notes on "The Killers", p. 48). Nick, however, whose innocence we feel, is still Adam before the fall.

(The name "Bugs" has a suggestive connotation, too: a bug is, originally, a blood-sucking insect, a parasite [!], a "big bug" is a term used to refer to an important person [cf. Bugs' living "like a gentleman"]. The name Bugs is also reminiscent of "bugger", a slang word used as a vulgar term of abuse; "buggered" means "spoilt, ruined"; in legal language a bugger is a sodomite, which would support the opinion of those who interpret the weird relationship between the soft-spoken, motherly Bugs and the ambivalent Ad as homosexual.)
Can we take it for granted that the sadly ironical title of the story, "The Battler" refers to Ad Francis alone? Or does it also refer to young Nick and his active engagement in the struggle of life?

The Result of Nick's Experience. Has Nick learnt anything from his meeting with the "Battler" and Bugs? What is different for him now? This type of question is hard to answer, as Hemingway's factual style presents mainly what is seen, not what is going on inside the characters.

We can assume that Nick has learnt, or is beginning to understand, that life holds confusing paradoxes, that people and situations cannot be taken at face value, that appearances can be deceptive, human behaviour irrational and often inexplicable. His naive trust in "champions" will have been shaken considering the ruinous after-effects of the example he has met. He may have realised that there are not only swamps and impenetrable forests in nature, but that in one's life, too, it is easy enough to lose the firm ground under one's feet and to get lost in the intricacies and wilderness of human passions and irrationalities. Nick has come into contact with yet another aspect of life which he cannot fully digest. He has taken one step further in his initiation into the world and lifestyles of the adults – a world that he is still too young to entirely comprehend.

Hemingway's View of Life in "The Battler". How, then, does Hemingway present life in this story? In a harsh, unfriendly setting Hemingway depicts episodes showing brutal, ugly, hostile aspects of life. There is no beauty in this story. The situations described (freight train journey, embankment hike, forest clearing and fire episode) are all utterly devoid of any romantic embellishment. Hemingway shows hard, realistic facts. What is lacking almost completely in this story is a female element, love. One woman is mentioned, though, but she is an ambivalent figure and Ad's relationship with her ended in "disagreement", failure. Her place is now filled by Bugs, the suave, polite Negro, who was in prison for stabbing a man with his knife!

Hemingway presents the experience of being beaten; variations on the theme of human violence, battling, craziness. The introductry story strikes the key-note with Nick's being knocked off the train he was travelling on; his cautious hike along the track and his careful approach to the fire signal Nick's constant awareness of danger and his fear of a sudden attack; Ad's interest in the brakeman, and then his bragging about beating all his opponents continues the main theme; his subsequent vicious attack on Nick and his own knock-out exemplify it further, and it dominates even in Bugs' talk about the unconscious fighter. This variation of a theme is reflected in the choice of verbs used: above all in the frequently repeated "bust" and "beat", but also in "hit", "knock", "tap", "thump"; all monosyllabic, hard, tough fighter's words. And of course the title "The Battler" sums it up neatly, too.

Ad's and Bugs' mutually interdependent existence, hiding from people, secreting themselves away in the wilderness, is a weird and disquieting portrayal of human lifestyles. But in this manner Hemingway reveals "toughness", fighting, and "taking a beating" as a questionable way of handling situations and of dealing with one's fellow human beings. Fast fists and slow hearts don't make it in the end!

Unterrichtsschritt 5:
Hemingway's Language and Style in "The Battler"

Depending on how much time the teacher wants to allot to a stylistic analysis of the short story, this point may vary greatly in length, and student projects might be included.

The students will note, as in the previously discussed stories, that Hemingway's language is seemingly simple, straightforward, realistic, everyday language, with a great deal of slang and colloquialisms in it. The major part of the story consists of dialogue.

□ Possible student project: *See how Hemingway manages the dialogue form.*

Hemingway uses very few directions; there are either no introductory or interpolative phrases at all, or merely the word "said"; there is hardly any variation. He strictly limits himself to letting the reader know who is speaking; *how* the characters say what they are saying is not explicitly described. This means, too, that we are hardly ever told anything about Nick's inner reactions and feelings, or those of the other two characters.

□ Possible student project: *Find out where in the text of the short story there is explicit mention or description of the characters' emotional reactions.*

Hemingway makes us draw our own conclusions from what is factually presented; we must learn constantly to read between and behind the lines, trying to catch the implications of what is said or described. In "Death in the Afternoon" Hemingway writes: "If a writer of prose knows enough about what he is writing about he may omit things that he knows, and the reader, if the writer is writing truly enough, will have a feeling of those things as strongly as though the writer had stated them. The dignity of movement of an iceberg is due to only one-eighth of it being above water." (Death in the Afternoon, p. 192.)

Something else will be noticed by the students: there are many repetitions of words (and of whole phrases) in the story, and, surprisingly, there is a lot of alliteration in the text.

□ Possible student project: *Study Hemingway's use of alliteration in this story. Pay particular attention to words beginning with "b".*

It is interesting to note Hemingway's choice of words beginning with the same consonant, such as *hit, hard, hurt,* and the effect achieved thereby. This analysis is especially rewarding if one studies the most frequently repeated words in "The Battler" that begin with a "b". The letter "b" is normally considered a "soft" sound. However, it will be noticed that most of the words beginning with the explosive "b" either have, or gain, an aggressive quality: cf. **B**attler, **b**eat, **b**eatings, **b**astard → **b**usted, **B**ugs, **b**rakeman, (Ad's muscles) **b**ulged a**b**ove the **b**one, (**B**ugs) **b**roke eggs. (Ad is knocked down with) a **b**lackjack, (the water) **b**elow shows **b**lack **b**etween the ties of the **b**ridge, Nick's **b**oots ring hollow. In fact even the **b**read in the central episode might be mentioned, as Nick's cutting the bread triggers off Ad's fit. It seems as if these words with initial "b" are expressive of **b**rutality and danger, and this effect is stressed further by Hemingway's frequent use of alliteration.

Unterrichtsschritt 6:
Weiterführende Fragestellungen

An die erwähnten sprachlichen Beobachtungen könnte sich die Frage nach typischen Merkmalen einer Short Story anschließen. Es würde genügen, einige Begriffe wie *episodic, limited number of persons, great concentration, sudden (open) beginning, open ending* zusammentragen zu lassen und eventuell über den *point of view* zu sprechen, aus dem heraus die Geschichte berichtet wird. Eine detaillierte Analyse der Gattung Short Story sollte allerdings einem späteren Stadium (Klasse 12 oder 13) vorbehalten bleiben. Weitere Möglichkeiten, das Thema dieser Kurzgeschichte weiter auszuschöpfen, ergäben sich aus Verknüpfungen und Vergleichen mit anderen Hemingway-Kurzgeschichten, z. B. mit "Indian Camp" und "The Killers".

Eine besonders fordernde und aufregende Aufgabenstellung sei zum Schluß angeregt: *creative writing.* Lassen Sie Ihre Schüler – ggfls. auf freiwilliger Basis – eine Fortsetzung von Nicks Erlebnissen schreiben, also ihre eigene Initiation Story!

Old Man at the Bridge

"Old Man at the Bridge" ist mit 762 Wörtern eine der kürzesten Short Stories, die Hemingway geschrieben hat. Sie entstand 1938 in Spanien, wo Hemingway als Kriegsberichterstatter im spanischen Bürgerkrieg tätig war.

Inmitten der Hektik eines den Ebro auf einer Behelfsbrücke überquerenden Flüchtlingsstroms sitzt ein alter Mann, verstaubt, am Rande des Weges und kann nicht weiter. Ein Soldat, wahrscheinlich im Range eines Offiziers, bemerkt den Alten. Nachdem er von einer Inspektion des Brückenkopfes über die Brücke zurückgekehrt ist, wechselt er ein paar Sätze mit ihm. Der alte Mann war von einem Hauptmann in San Carlos aufgefordert worden, sich vor der anrückenden Artillerie in Sicherheit zu bringen. Als letzter war er gegangen, hatte schweren Herzens seine Tiere zurückgelassen. Zwölf Kilometer hat er geschafft, bis über die Pontonbrücke, aber an der steilen Böschung auf der anderen Seite kann er nicht mehr weiter. Während nach und nach der Flüchtlingsstrom versiegt und der Angriff des Feindes unmittelbar bevorsteht, versucht der Offizier, den alten Mann zum Weitergehen zu veranlassen. Doch dessen Kräfte versagen. "There was nothing to do about him."

Hemingway gestaltet mit wenigen Sätzen ein beinahe archetypisches menschliches Schicksal, indem die Sinnlosigkeit des Krieges mit dem Ende eines friedlichen, harmlosen alten Mannes, dessen ganze Sorge und Fürsorge ein paar Tieren gegolten hat, beispielhaft beleuchtet wird. Trotz der Zeichnung einiger individueller Züge gewinnen der alte Mann und der Offizier somit etwas Exemplarisches.

Zum methodischen Vorgehen

Zweifellos kann "Old Man at the Bridge" gelesen und verstanden werden, ohne daß im Detail auf den spanischen Bürgerkrieg eingegangen wird. Einige wenige skizzierende Hinweise würden genügen. Das Exemplarische des Geschehens bedarf nicht der historisch-vordergründigen Einzelheiten.

Andererseits jedoch bietet sich gerade im Zusammenhang mit dieser Kurzgeschichte ein interessanter Umweg an, der zugleich eine methodische Variante zum üblichen Vorgehen bei der Textarbeit darstellt. Hemingway verfolgte mit großer Anteilnahme den spanischen Bürgerkrieg und stand ganz auf der Seite der Republikaner. Seit Februar 1937 erlebte er die Kämpfe in Spanien sogar selbst als Kriegsberichterstatter mit, und infolgedessen gibt es von ihm viele Berichte über die Vorgänge in Spanien, die er an seine Zeitung durchgegeben hat. Es lohnt sich daher, die Schüler als Einstieg einmal einen solchen *dispatch* lesen zu lassen, der inhaltlich in engem historischen Zusammenhang mit der Kurzgeschichte steht (die Hemingway übrigens auch zunächst aus Barcelona als Bericht an seine Zeitung gekabelt hatte!).

Wenn dieser methodische Zwischenschritt eingelegt wird, so muß allerdings – entweder durch Lehrerinformation oder durch ein Schülerkurzreferat – ein Minimum an Informationen über den Spanischen Bürgerkrieg (und auch über den Anteil Hitlers an diesem Konflikt) geliefert werden. Der vorgeschaltete Kriegsbericht "The Bombing of Tortosa" vom 15. 4. 1938 (vgl. S. 70/71) wird gewiß Neugier und Interesse wecken, sollte jedoch hauptsächlich als Folie für die folgende Besprechung der Short Story dienen. Wiewohl Hemingways Kriegsbericht sich durchaus nicht trocken liest, wird die anschließende Lektüre von "Old Man at the Bridge" den Schülern die ungeheuer verdichtete Sprache der Short Story desto deutlicher bewußt machen.

Aufgabenstellung zur 1. Stunde

Die Schüler bekommen den Text "The Bombing of Tortosa" vervielfältigt ausgehändigt. Dazu erhalten sie folgende Aufgaben:
a) Read Hemingway's cabled war report "The Bombing of Tortosa" (Apr. 15, 1938) and look up the words you don't know.
b) Get a map of Spain, look up the course of the Ebro river, and find Tortosa and the other cities mentioned.
c) Answer the following questions:
   1. What two bombings are described in the first three paragraphs of the dispatch?
   2. What types and makes of planes are mentioned? Do the names tell you anything?
   3. Comment on the style in which this war report is written. (Is this what you would have expected of a typical war report? If not, in what respect does it differ?)

Ein Schüler (bzw. ein Team von Schülern) erhält die Aufgabe, ein Kurzreferat über den spanischen Bürgerkrieg anzufertigen und (möglichst frei) zu Beginn der folgenden Stunde vorzutragen.
(*Alternative:* Lehrervortrag und/oder *handout* zum Spanischen Bürgerkrieg.)

1. Stunde:
The Bombing of Tortosa

Unterrichtsschritt 1:
The Spanish Civil War

In einem kurzen Referat berichtet ein Schüler (ggfls. als Sprecher einer Arbeitsgruppe) über die Ursachen und Gründe des spanischen Bürgerkrieges (1936–39), über die beiden Seiten, die sich feindlich gegenüberstanden, über Verlauf und Ausgang des Krieges. Die Unterstützung der Falangisten (= Faschisten) durch Hitler und Mussolini sollte erwähnt werden. Als Beispiel für das militärische Eingreifen Hitlers kann die Entsendung der Legion Condor dienen, die z. B. wesentlich an der völligen Zerstörung der Stadt Guernica beteiligt war. (Verweis auf das berühmte Bild Picassos!) Sollten keine Geschichtsbücher mit hinreichenden Informationen zur Verfügung stehen, so könnte ein Schüler zumindest den Inhalt der "Historical Facts and Figures on the Spanish Civil War" (vgl. S. 69) referieren. Es wäre sinnvoll, wenn das Kurzreferat durch ein Folienbild oder *handout,* zumindest aber durch einen Tafelanschrieb gestützt würde (→ T 1)

Unterrichtsschritt 2:
Hemingway's Engagement in the Spanish Civil War

The teacher should say a few sentences about Hemingway's involvement in the Spanish Civil War. Hemingway was a passionate supporter of the Republican side and tried to help as best he could to fight the Fascists. He took part in some fund-raising in order to provide the Republicans with medical equipment, and in February 1937 went to Spain as a war correspondent. He spent a lot of time in Spain until the end of the war.

Some Historical Facts and Figures on the Spanish Civil War

The Republic of Spain was held under the military dictatorship of General Primo de Rivera from 1923 to 1930. In the anarchy that followed de Rivera's resignation, the Republicans obtained a majority in the local elections. King Alfonso was exiled, and
5 the Second Spanish Republic formally came into being on Dec. 9, 1931; a typical parliamentary democracy.

In the following four and a half years there were three changes of Government (Liberals / Conservatives / Popular Front coalition). The Popular Front proclaimed a mildly Socialist policy of land reform and some measure of State intervention with
10 regard to industry. The conservative elements were opposed to this, attacked the government, and on July 18, 1936 attempted to seize power by a coup d'état. The leader of this military rebellion was General Franco. The government raised an army strong enough to oppose the rebels for two and a half years in a terrible civil war.

At the beginning of the Civil War the parties were clearly defined. On the one side
15 were those opposed to the Republican ideal, although they did not necessarily favour a restoration of the monarchy (the "Monarchists", landowners, the Roman Catholic Church, businessmen). They valued above all the preservation of authority, order and discipline, and supported the revolutionary army, whose avowed purpose was "to save Spain from Bolshevism". This "Nationalist" party, led by General Franco,
20 received immediate material support from Germany and Italy, the first German planes arriving 10 days after the rebellion.

On the other side were the Republicans (Liberals, Socialists, Communists, Basque Nationalists); they received some help from Russia, and from volunteers all over the world. (However, it was estimated that 10,000 Germans and 70,000 Italians were
25 serving with the Nationalists by Spring 1937, whereas only 2000 Russians, mainly airmen and technicians, were serving with the Spanish Republican Army.)

The Spanish Republican Government continued to struggle until March 1939, but the amount of assistance which Germany and Italy were openly giving to the Nationalist side brought about the victory of General Franco's party, after a slow but steady
30 subjugation of the whole country by the rebel forces. The Spanish Civil War ended with the surrender of Madrid on March 30, 1939. General Franco, the "Caudillo" (= leader), became the head of a regime patterned after those of Mussolini and Hitler.

Based on: A. J. Grant/H. Temperley, Europe in the 19th and 20th Centuries, London, Longmans 1962[6]
and: R. Albrecht-Carrié, Europe After 1815, Littlefield, Paterson N. J. 1962[3]

The Bombing of Tortosa

Tortosa, Spain. – Ahead of us fifteen Heinkel light bombers, protected by Messerschmidt pursuit planes, swung 'round and 'round in a slow circle, like vultures waiting for an animal to die. Each time they passed over a certain point, there was the thud of bombs. As they swung over the bare hillside, keeping their steady formation,
5 every third ship would dive, its guns spitting. They kept that up for forty-five minutes unmolested and what they were diving and bombing on was a company of infantry making a last stand on the hillside and bare ridge at noon on this hot spring day to defend the Barcelona–Valencia road.

Above us in the high cloudless sky, fleet after fleet of bombers roared over Tortosa.
10 When they dropped the sudden thunder of their loads, the little city on the Ebro disappeared in a yellow mounting cloud of dust. The dust never settled, as more bombers came, and, finally, it hung like a yellow fog all down the Ebro valley. The big Savoia-Marchetti bombers shone white and silvery in the sun, and, as one group hammered over, another came.

15 Ahead of us all this time, the Heinkels were circling and diving with the mechanical monotony of movement of a quiet afternoon at a six-day bike race. And, under them, a company of men lay behind rocks in hastily dug fox holes and in simple folds of the ground, trying to hold up the advance of an army.

At midnight, the government communiqué admitted there was fighting around San
20 Mateo and La Jana, which meant the last big defensive position, La Tancada, a steep rocky hill defending the road to the sea from Morella to Vinaroz, had been turned or taken.

At 4 o'clock in the morning, driving into a full moon that lighted the rocky Catalan hills, the jutting cypresses and weirdly chopped trunks of the plane trees, we headed
25 for the front. By daylight we passed the old Roman walls of Tarragona, and, by the time the sun was warming, we were meeting the first groups of refugees.

Later, we met troops who told of the break-through and that two columns were advancing on Vinaroz, a third on Ulldecona and a fourth from Lacenia toward La Galera in the direction of Santa Barbara, which is only thirteen kilometers from
30 Tortosa. It was a four-fingered push toward the sea by General Aranda's column of Navarrese troops and Moors, and officers reported it had already taken Calig and San Jorge, the last two towns on the two roads from San Mateo toward the sea.

At 1 o'clock this afternoon, the road was still open, but all signs pointed toward its being cut or brought under artillery fire by tonight or as soon as Aranda's troops could
35 bring up their guns. Meantime, from where this correspondent was talking in Ulldecona with a staff officer, his maps spread out on a stone wall, he could hear the firing of the machine guns.

The staff officer was talking coolly, carefully and with great politeness while Aranda's troops were advancing past San Rafael, with only one ridge left between them and us.
40 He was a very brave and competent soldier and was ordering up his armored cars, but our car wasn't armored, so we decided to return past Santa Barbara. It was a nice little town, but it would have been better except that Tortosa was still spouting clouds of smoke as the bombers unloaded.

There were many reasons impelling us to get by Tortosa toward Barcelona, including
45 life, liberty and the pursuit of happiness. So when the car arrived at Tortosa and a
guard said the bombers had blown up the bridge and that we couldn't go through, it
was something that we had worried about for so long and so many times it made
almost no impression except a feeling that "now it has really happened."
"You can try the little bridge that they are fixing with some planks," the guard said.
50 The chauffeur jumped the car forward, threaded through a line of trucks, past bomb
holes into which two trucks could drop out of sight in the still freshly scorched earth
and the acrid high-explosive smell, and on to the little bridge. Ahead was a mule cart.
"You can't go there," the guard shouted to the peasant leading the cart, heavily laden
with grain, household goods, cooking pots, a jug of wine, and all the mule could haul
55 with difficulty. But the mule had no reverse and the bridge was blocked. So your
correspondent pushed on the wheels, the peasant hauled on the mule's head and the
cart rolled slowly forward, followed by the car, the narrow ironshod cart-wheels
smashing the too-light new crossroads that kids were nailing down in a rush to get the
frail bridge ready for traffic.
60 The boys were working, hammering, nailing and sawing as fast and hard as a good
crew on a vessel in distress at sea. And, on our right, one section of the great iron
bridge across the Ebro had slumped down into the stream and another gaped missing.
The mass bombing of forty-eight bombers, using bombs, judging from the holes they
made and the way they flung houses into rubble across the road, which must have
65 been between 300 and 450 pounds apiece, had got the Tortosa bridge at last. In the
town, a gasoline truck was burning. Driving through the street was like mountaineering in the craters of the moon. The railroad bridge still stands and a pontoon bridge
undoubtedly will be built, but it is a bad night for the west bank of the Ebro.

NANA Dispatch April 15, 1938
Aus: W. White, ed., By-Line: Ernest Hemingway. Selected Articles and Dispatches of Four
Decades, Charles Scribner's Sons, New York 1967, p. 284–286.

Unterrichtsschritt 3:
The Bombing of Tortosa

The pupils read the war report out in three parts: ll. 1–18; 19–43; 44–68. The text should then be discussed relatively quickly, incorporating the guiding questions the pupils had to answer as their homework. Factual details are of less interest than the manner of presentation of the war report.

Hemingway describes two bombings in his report, clearly distinguished by his introductory "ahead of us" and "above us". Ahead of the reporter, on the hillside, a company of infantry is being mercilessly bombarded and shot at, the soldiers seeking shelter behind rocks in hastily dug holes. And above the reporter an incessant fleet of heavy bombers drop their load onto Tortosa. The bombing of Tortosa constitutes the typical war-time attack on cities; however, the "unmolested" 45 minutes machine-gun fire attack on the helplessly hiding infantry seems to imply a good deal of masochistic brutality. (Cf. the comparison of the planes with "vultures waiting for an animal to die".)

The Heinkel light bombers and the Messerschmidt pursuit planes are German planes and most likely manned by German crews as well. Hitler's support of the Spanish Falangists (= Fascists) was downright material, and he sent in part of the German airforce (known as the "Condor Legion"). The Savoia-Marchetti bombers are Italian planes. (Italy's Fascist leader, Mussolini, was also sending vast supplies of arms and planes in support of Franco's Falangists.)

The war correspondent (Hemingway) is heading for the front for two reasons: on the one hand he wants to report from the immediate war theatre and thus talks to the staff officer (l. 36ff.) within hearing range of the enemy machine guns ("with only one ridge left between them and us"); on the other hand he hopes to sneak through one of the last loop-holes in the front and to escape towards Barcelona, where he would be in safety.

It is interesting to take a closer look at the style in which this report is written.

Surely, a war report can be expected to deliver brief, concise, crisp, factual information. Does Hemingway's report comply with this kind of expectation? His dispatch on the bombing of Tortosa is a reporter's eye-witness account, and, indeed, full of realistic and circumstantial details. The account is structured to a certain extent by the times mentioned ("at noon on this hot spring day" – "At midnight" – "at 4 o'clock" – "by daylight" – "later" – "at one o'clock"). It is seemingly straightforward and yet there are a number of points that go beyond a matter-of-fact war report.

– It is a very *personal* report. The correspondent uses the personal pronouns "we", "us" throughout. He is personally involved; the story of the bombing of Tortosa is *his* story as well. (Cf. especially ll. 44–48!) (Maybe the students will notice that very occasionally Hemingway changes from "us" and "we" to "this correspondent" and "he" (l. 35ff.).

– The report goes beyond factual description when landscapes or situational details are described. (Cf. the almost impressionist details in the description of the trees, l. 24f., or the mule cart episode, l. 52ff.) It seems as though Hemingway just can't help using descriptive adjectives.

– Hemingway sometimes makes striking poetic comparisons, uses similes. (Reference possible to Arbeitsblatt Literary Terms, p. 79.) Thus, the circling bombers are compared to "vultures" (l. 2f.), and driving through the street in Tortosa is compared to "mountaineering in the craters of the moon" (l. 66). The mechanical circling and diving of the planes is compared to the regularity and monotony of a six-day bike race (l. 15f.). This last example is typical of yet another characteristic of Hemingway's style in this dispatch.

– Hemingway's report contains a good deal of (rather bitter) irony. After all, the deadly routine circling of bomber planes and the six-day cycling routine have nothing in common but the circular movement. When (in l. 44ff.) Hemingway mentions "many reasons to get by Tortosa to Barcelona including life, liberty and the pursuit of happiness" he ironically quotes the famous words of the Declaration of Independence, referring implicitly to his own wish to escape unscathed. And there is good-natured irony (in l. 55ff.) when "your correspondent" helps the peasant with his cart, as "the mule had no reverse..."

Conclusion: Hemingways' war report is not restricted to sober facts and figures, but rather it is a lively, descriptive account that clearly bears the author's handwriting.

Die Schüler sollen nun Hemingways Short Story "Old Man at the Bridge" lesen. Die historisch-inhaltliche Nähe der Kurzgeschichte zum Kriegsbericht einerseits und der formale Kontrast zu ihr andererseits wird die Schüleraufmerksamkeit für die kompositorische Geschlossenheit und die größere sprachliche Dichte von "Old Man at the Bridge" schärfen. Die drei mitgegebenen Leitfragen (vgl. Stundenblatt) sollen diesen Erkenntnisprozeß fördern.

2. Stunde:
The Opening Situation / The Officer

Unterrichtsschritt 1:
Textvortrag

Zu Beginn der Stunde hört die Klasse den Text der Kurzgeschichte entweder vom Band ("Old Man at the Bridge" findet sich auf der Toncassette, Klett Nr. 50897, zu Modern Life, Revised Edition, Sprechdauer 4'42") oder als Lehrervortrag, eventuell auch von einem guten (auf den Vortrag vorbereiteten) Schüler gelesen.

Unterrichtsschritt 2:
Kurzer Vergleich zwischen War Report und "Old Man at the Bridge"

After reading Hemingway's war report in the previous lesson with the intention of having it serve as a foil and point of reference for the short story, the aim now is to point out, without any great loss of time, the basic difference between a text that just reports a number of interesting and moving facts, and a literary text that is marked by a most carefully structured composition, by its choice of words, and by its selection of exemplary characters. Whether the formal aspect, or that of content is touched on first, is irrelevant.

The basic difference, as far as the content of the two texts goes, is that although both texts deal with principally the same war situation, Hemingway in his short story singles out one human fate, one striking situation, to epitomize the helplessness of the innocent individual, and ultimately, the senselessness of the sacrifice of human life in wars. In Hemingway's war report the disastrous bombing of the city and of the soldiers in their foxholes is much more anonymous, is seen from greater distance, as it were; it seems to be taken for granted that people suffer and die in the process of war. Formally, the difference is equally obvious: whereas the war report is written in narrative, descriptive prose, the short story is strongly determined by dialogue. The report contains a relatively loosely ordered account, basically following the time sequence of the day (at midnight / at 4 o'clock / by daylight / etc.); the short story is carefully structured, is marked by meaningful contrasts and functional repetitions. Every word counts. The headline of the dispatch refers to a specific wartime situation, *the bombing* of Tortosa, whereas the omission of the definite article in the title of the short story "*Old Man* at the Bridge" points at the almost generic significance of the old refugee's fate.

Unterrichtsschritt 3:
The Opening Situation of "Old Man at the Bridge"

As Hemingway's short story "Old Man at the Bridge" is not only one of his shortest but also one of his most complex stories, it is mandatory to have a clear methodical approach for its interpretation. The method suggested here is to discuss the opening section first, then talk about the officer (narrator), and finally concentrate on the old man as the central figure of this story. Obviously, a certain amount of overlapping is unavoidable in class discussion. Hemingway's "Old Man at the Bridge" would best be discussed in a double period.

It is necessary to take a very close look at the situation that is described in just seven lines at the opening of the short story, and it will help to make a simple board diagram (→ T 2) to clarify some of the details (such as the pontoon = makeshift floating bridge, the steep bank of the Ebro river and the steep hill, the bridgehead on the other (= Western) side, the place by the side of the road where the old man is sitting, etc.).

One important detail which is sometimes missed by students is that the old man has already crossed the bridge and is now sitting on the Eastern side. (This is clear from the second paragraph.)

Do we know why the old man is sitting by the side of the road? Of course, we are aware of the background (Spanish Civil War) and realize that the old man must be a refugee. But would we have known without any background information? Where in the text is there a first suggestion that we are dealing with a war situation? It is the mention of a special type of bridge, the pontoon bridge, because such a bridge is made up of flat boats in cases of war time emergencies. And there is a sense of emergency about this scene when we hear that "carts, trucks, and men, women and children" are crossing it. Then "soldiers" are mentioned who help push the carts up the steep bank, and the trucks that head "out of it all". (Immediately afterwards the words "bridgehead" and "enemy advancing" make the flight situation absolutely clear.)

Once again, Hemingway puts the reader right into a situation, and leaves it to him to respond to the suggestions the text contains.

The opening passage is determined by a marked contrast between the movement and activity of the refugees escaping from danger (cf. the verbs: *stagger, push, grind up and away, head out of it, plod*) and the immobility of the old man sitting by the road of whom we are told: " He was too tired to go any further." This contrast between flight, movement, action on the one hand and rest, motionlessness on the other should be noted down in a board diagram (→ T 3). (In the course of the story the hustle and activity around the old man will decrease, as fewer and fewer carts and people come over the bridge and move away to safety, until in the end he is the only civilian left, too exhausted to walk any further, sinking back into the dust of the road.)

Unterrichtsschritt 4:
The Officer

Not clear from the start, but becoming obvious from the beginning of the second paragraph, the situation is described by a narrator, a soldier, most likely of the rank of an officer, as may be concluded from the second paragraph. He has come to the bridge to inspect the fortified bridgehead on the other side of the river (which has been set up to try and stop the advancing enemy). From the factual way he briefly refers to his "business" stating briskly and precisely what he had to do ("to cross . . . to explore . . . fo find out") we can discern an unemotional attitude of military precision and alertness. (→ T 4) Before, on his way across the bridge, he was observant of the continuous stream of refugees, mule-carts, peasants, trucks and all, and also aware of the old man whose immobility was marking such an obvious contrast.

Now, after returning from his tour of inspection he notices that there are fewer carts and very few people on foot, "but the old man was still there." (This line corresponds with: "But the old man sat there without moving." and later "and the old man still sat there".)

Now that his attention is drawn to the old man, he starts a friendly chat, asks where he comes from, and shows some interest in him. However, he seems only mildly interested in the old man, doesn't quite understand his explanation, and responds with a rather non-committal "oh". However, he does take a closer look at him (at his dusty clothes, his grey, dusty face, his simple steelrimmed spectacles) and puts yet another question. But all this time his main attention is elsewhere: he is watching the bridge, waiting for the first signs of the enemy. (Note the choice of words in: "watching the bridge... wondering how long now... listening all the while...") His soldier's nerves are all keyed to sensing "the first noises that would signal that ever mysterious event called contact", words that characterize the narrator as one to whom fighting is a "mysterious" and probably exciting process. So intent is the officer on watching the bridge and the surrounding countryside that he seems to have missed the old man's answer to his question, "What animals were they?", and he repeats the question.

The narrator's further questions, although quite sympathetic, are very much on a conversational level ("And you had to leave them?", "And you have no family?"), his answers obliging, but all this while the old man does not have his undivided attention. The officer keeps watching the far end of the bridge and takes notice of the fact that now "a few last carts were hurrying down the slope of the bank." The effect on the reader of the carts being mentioned several times (evacuating refugees) is one of increasing tension, of time running out, a heightened sense of danger. When eventually the officer – still watching the far bank – states "now there were no carts", we know that the "mysterious event called contact" is imminent!

Sympathetic though the officer is, and trying to help the old man (just like that captain in San Carlos who told the old man to leave his home town, warning him of the artillery) he does not concentrate his attention enough on the old man to really help him. Although he realizes when he first sees him that the old man is "too tired to go any farther", and although the old man stresses this fact when he says "I can go no farther" the officer does not simply stop one of the carts and put him on it. Instead, he waits till it is too late and there are no more carts to turn to for help. And – with his mind still absorbed with the advancing enemy – he finally resigns himself to a fatalistic "There was nothing to do about him." The question whether the officer in his distracted conversation with the old man really understands the old man now shifts our attention to the actual protagonist.

(If no double period is available for the discussion of "Old Man at the Bridge" the question "Does the officer really understand the old man?" might be put as homework for the next class.)

3. Stunde:
The Old Man

Unterrichtsschritt 1:
Does the Officer Understand the Old Man?

Does the officer really understand the old man? To answer this question we must take another look at the conversation between the two men. We will realize that the officer doesn't show any direct emotional reaction in this encounter, so we can't really say much about his feelings. Also, as we noticed before, his main attention is focused on the advancing enemy so that his part in the dialogue is rather laconic and very much "conversational". And yet it will become clear that the officer gives the old man enough of his attention to interpret some of his reactions correctly (for instance, when he realizes that the old man smiles because it gives him pleasure to mention his home town.) However, he seems to fail to understand the old man's real problem, namely that having to leave his home and his animals has so completely uprooted him that his attempted flight (prompted by the captain and probably not completely understood in all its consequences by the old man himself) is bound to lead to his complete mental and physical disintegration. Also the officer doesn't quite understand the old man's concern for his animals; when the old man keeps on musing about his animals' fate the officer concludes "And you have no family?" and then tries to change the subject with his question about the old man's political convictions. The old man's overwhelmingly simple answer "I am without politics. I am seventy-six years old. I have come twelve kilometres now and I think I can go no farther." seems to have touched the officer, because he suddenly urges the old man to move on up the road, towards Tortosa and Barcelona. "This is not a good place to stop", he comments with some understatement. But then he fails to understand the sad implication of the old man's words that he doesn't know anyone "in that direction".

The old man probably spent his whole life in San Carlos and that is where his thoughts return, because he left his animals behind there. The officer realizes how worried the old man is about the animals, but when the old man "having to share his worry with someone" suddenly asks him a question about the animals' fate, the officer's answers reveal – if not some irritation – at least a very off-handed, superficial attitude ("Why, they'll probably come through it all right. – Why not?"). Or could the officer in fact have realized the reason for the old man's worry and is he trying to convey some

optimism here, in order to console the old man and to put his mind at rest? That would also explain his remark about the pigeons (he calls them doves!) – "they'll fly."

However, the old man cannot be consoled; there are still the other animals, the goats... Again, as though he had been moved by the old man's deep and genuine concern for the handful of animals entrusted to his care, the officer urges the old man to get up and try to walk on, only to realize that, indeed, "there was nothing to do about him," now. Whether or not the officer really understands, whether or not he can fathom the reason for the old man's worry and the ultimate cause of his suffering, cannot be finally decided. However, we can define the function of the narrator now: the officer serves as a foil against which the real protagonist of the story, the old man, is seen the more clearly. By contrast with the officer, the pathetic fate of the old man comes out distinctly.

Unterrichtsschritt 2:
The Old Man Contrasted With the Officer

In a brief repetition, the main characteristics that have been found out about the officer should be listed in a board diagram, to be contrasted with those of the old man ($\rightarrow$ T 5). The officer's age can only be guessed; he is a soldier on the Republican side, war is his business, and although he takes some interest in the old man by the roadside his main attention is devoted to the advancing enemy artillery.

The old man is different in every respect. He sits motionless in all the rushing activity of the refugees' flight, an isolated, solitary figure. He is 76 years of age and has no family, and – he is "without politics". What are the implications of these strangely rudimentary words? The old man has no part in this conflict between Fascists and Republicans, he is too old, and maybe too limited, to see through political arguments, and consequences. The narrowly circumscribed circle of his life is outlined by the name of his home town, San Carlos, where he was born (cf. "native town") and where he probably spent his whole life, until he was told by the captain to leave, "because of the artillery". Artillery here stands as a synonym for war, the threatening guns as a symbol of peace-destroying, life-uprooting forces.

He "was only taking care of animals" – this sentence, repeated several times, epitomizes the tragic situation. We can easily picture a peaceful rural scene with the old man and the animals, reminiscent perhaps of Francis of Assisi. The word that stands out is *Care,* and it strangely and ominously contrasts with the word *War* (which though not directly mentioned in the story is implied in the bridgehead situation throughout). This harmless old man whose only concern were two goats, a cat, and four pairs of pigeons, was made to leave home and animals in order to save his life (he was the last to leave!); but his thoughts keep centering around the animals he left behind. Typically enough, he is worried about *their* fate, not about *his*. There is a certain amount of naiveté, or shall we say innocence, about him when he muses about his animals. He appreciates the fact that the cat will be all right, "A cat can look out for itself."

Maybe the students could be alerted at this point to the symbolic significance of the animals mentioned. They could be asked to state the associations they have when they think of "cats, pigeons, goats". They will probably repeat the general notion that cats "always fall on their feet", are clever, enduring, "have nine lives", are relatively independent. (They sneak away when someone throws a stone at them, just as the refugees run away from impending danger and purposefully head for safety. They will be "all right" under the circumstances.) And

pigeons, or "doves" as the officer says? Clearly, they are a symbol of peace and love, – and the picture of the artillery firing at them is in itself a most powerful symbol that needs no further comment. And the goats? The students will probably see the goats as a source of nourishment. Goats give milk that can be turned into cheese. Milk and cheese are essentials of life; here they are destroyed in the war. Moreover, however, the goats evoke associations with Greek tragedy, with tragic sacrifice and human suffering. The goat (Greek "tragos") is the animal that was sacred to Dionysos, and the word "tragedy" is derived from it (tragos + odia = tragoidia, meaning goat-song).

Without pushing the symbolic significance of the old man's animals too far, a few parallels can, no doubt, be drawn. Obviously the old man is not like the cat; he cannot look after himself any longer. Is he like the pigeons then, which he left behind with their cage door open? They have a chance to fly out and escape into safety, just as the old man has managed to cross the bridge, the door to safety seems open...

But a realistic assessment of the situation will come to the conclusion that the pigeons will probably not get away from the artillery fire, just like the old man who can't go any farther and hasn't got much of a chance now.

Maybe the goats ("... the others. It's better not to think of the others") provide the clearest hint at the old man's fate: they, like the old man, are helpless, innocent, guiltless and yet made to suffer. Instead of living their simple, peaceful existence, of giving milk for nourishing food, the goats will be slaughtered in a senseless war. The old man, too, helpless, innocent, guiltless as he is, is made to suffer from a conflict he has no part in.

The flight from San Carlos does not only mean the loss of his home, it means the loss of his centre, and ultimately of his life. Having to leave his home is the beginning of the end for the old man. He has reached, and crossed the bridge (!), but there is no sense in his flight, as there is no goal for him to go towards. This war has pulled the ground away from under his feet and thus there is really "nothing to do about him." When in the end he sits backwards in the dust, we remember that the narrator mentions his "very dusty clothes" in the first line, we recall the long dusty road, the "black dusty clothes" and "his grey dusty face". When the old man sinks back into the dust the situation suggests the Biblical "ashes to ashes and dust to dust" and thus strongly evokes a premonition of the old man's death.

(In this connection the students' attention could be drawn to the kind of landscape that forms the background to this story: "African – looking", dusty, barren, hostile, in keeping with the spirit of a war situation.)

Unterrichtsschritt 3:
The Meaning of the Ending

In the very last paragraph of the short story, as though it didn't seem very important to him, the narrator almost coincidentally mentions the fact that this episode is happening on Easter Sunday. (He also identifies the enemy now as the Fascists, thus making it clear that he is on the Republican side.) What is not of great importance to the officer nevertheless assumes a deeper, ironical meaning to the reader. Easter Sunday, in Christian belief, is one of the most significant holidays in the church year, commemorating Christ's resurrection. The fact that Christ has risen from the tomb stands as a symbol of hope, redemption and salvation for mankind. In the face of this, the fact that the old man sinks back into the dust and cannot rise any more, might be interpreted as a bitter piece of irony ("tragic irony" even), the more so as the last line of the story also sounds rather sarcastic, almost heartless. The old man has no "good luck" in this situation but will perish as an innocent victim in a senseless war, a tragic symbol of the waste of human life. (If there is any salvation for him it will come to him after his death when according to the Christian faith those who suffer innocently will be redeemed.)

It is not clear what, if anything, the old man's impending death means to the officer. We don't know if his last remark is really sarcastic, or whether his seemingly superior and stoic attitude is only hiding the fact that he, too, has learnt something about the relativity of values, the futility of "politics", the immeasurable cost of war, through his contact (sic!) with the old man.

Vorschlag für ein Arbeitsblatt

Some literary terms

Ambiguity: [æmbi'gjuiti]	The deliberate use of a word or phrase that has two or more relevant meanings.
Alliteration:	The repetition of a letter or sound in subsequent words, usually at the beginning of a syllable, for special emphasis. (e. g.: "Her light laughter lifted his soul.")
Atmosphere:	The general mood which is established in a literary work by the setting, choice of words, imagery, and theme.
Character:	Person in a play, novel, or story. Hence: main character.
Characterization:	Direct or indirect description of a person and his or her typical qualities. Explicit characterization: the author makes a direct statement about the character (e. g.: Mary was happy and content.) Implicit characterization: the character does or says something, or others say something about him or her, from which the reader can draw the appropriate conclusions (e. g.: Mary's eyes were shining; she went home singing all the way.)
Climax:	The highest point of interest, the decisive moment in the action; the moment that determines whether the situation of the protagonist will improve or deteriorate. (Often the turning-point, too.) Hence: anti-climax: a sudden unexpected occurence that contrasts with a previous high degree of tension and causes it to drop.
Dénouement:	The outcome of the plot, the final resolution that brings the conflict, or the action, to an end.
Dramatic Irony:	A bitter contradiction between appearance and reality which is recognized by the reader of a story (or the spectator of a play), who sees a character acting in ignorance of his real situation. A character may confidently say something expecting the opposite of what fate holds in store for him; or he says something that unwittingly anticipates the tragic outcome.
Exposition:	The introduction to a story, the part in which the reader receives the background information necessary for an understanding of the plot. The setting and main characters are introduced, the atmosphere is established, and facts that the reader needs to know are supplied.
Flashback:	A passage in a narrative by which the chronological sequence of events is interrupted to deal with earlier scenes or events, illuminating the (hero's) past. (A technique frequently used in films.)

Image:	A figure of speech that brings a picture to mind. (e. g.: Clouds towering like mountains. A man who towers above his contemporaries.) Cf. simile, metaphor. Hence: imagery (dt. Bildersprache).
Metaphor: ['metəfə]	A word that indicates something different from its literal meaning (e. g.: He has a heart of gold.) Hence: metaphorical language: language containing metaphors.
Open Beginning:	The beginning of a story in the middle of an action without any introductory passage or explanation.
Open Ending:	The ending of a story without a final solution; the outcome is left open.
Paraphrase:	The rewording of a phrase or passage in the reader's own words, usually in a simpler and clearer form.
Plot:	The outline of the events of a story.
Protagonist:	The main character in a story or play; the "hero".
Setting:	The place and time in which the action takes place; the environment and background of the characters.
Simile: ['simili]	Comparison of one thing to another (e. g.: He is as brave as a lion. – She walks like an angel.)
Symbol:	A word or thing that stands significantly for something abstract, or some more comprehensive idea (e. g. The Cross is the symbol of Christianity.) Hence: symbolic of
Tension: ['tenʃn]	Condition when feelings are under great strain; the reader is kept in great suspense, waiting eagerly for what is going to happen. Tension is increased, or relaxed. Hence: curve of tension.
Turning-point:	The moment when the situation changes either for better or for worse.

Auswahlbibliographie

1. Basic Material

Hanneman, Audre: Ernest Hemingway. A Comprehensive Bibliography, Princeton 1967. Supplement, Princeton 1975 (A superb Hemingway bibliography to be consulted in all events.)

Sanderson, Stewart: Hemingway. (Writers and Critics, Vol. 7) Oliver and Boyd Ltd, Edinburgh 1961. (An excellent elementary study of Hemingway.)

Flora, Joseph: Hemingway's Nick Adams. Louisiana State Univ. Press, Baton Rouge and London 1982. (A good recent publication on Hemingway's Nick Adams stories.)

Goetsch, Paul (ed.): Studien und Materialien zur Short Story. Schule und Forschung Bd. 15, Diesterweg, Frankfurt 1971. (A good book on the American Short Story containing an excellent interpretation of Hemingway's "Old Man at the Bridge".)

2. For Further Reading

a) Ernest Hemingway

Baker, Carlos: Hemingway, The Writer as Artist, Princeton 1952, rev. ed. 1972[4].

Benson, Jackson, ed.: The Short Stories of Ernest Hemingway, Critical Essays, Durham, North Carolina 1975.

DeFalco, Joseph: The Hero in Hemingway's Short Stories, University of Pittsburgh Press 1963.

Grebstein, Sheldon N.: Hemingway's Craft, Carbondale and Edwardsville 1973.

Gurko, Leo: Ernest Hemingway and the Pursuit of Heroism, New York 1968.

Killinger, John: Hemingway and the Dead Gods, A Study in Existentialism, University of Kentucky Press 1960.

Laurence, Frank M.: Hemingway and the Movies, University Press of Mississippi, Jackson 1981.

Rovit, Earl: Ernest Hemingway, Twayne Publishers, Boston 1967.

Weber, Horst, ed.: Hemingway, Wege der Forschung Bd 546, Wiss. Buchges. Darmstadt 1980.

Young, Philip: Ernest Hemingway. A Reconsideration, repr. University Park 1968.

b) The American Short Story

Ahrends, Günter: Die amerikanische Kurzgeschichte, Theorie und Entwicklung, Kohlhammer Stuttgart, 1980.

Bungert, Hans, ed.: Die amerikanische Short Story, Wege der Forschung Bd. CCLVI, Wiss. Buchges. Darmstadt 1972 (darin vor allem der Aufsatz von H. Galinsky mit einer guten Interpretation von "The Killers").

Freese, Peter, ed.: Die amerikanische Short Story der Gegenwart, Berlin 1976.

Göller, K. H./Hoffmann, G, eds.: Die amerikanische Kurzgeschichte, Bagel Verl. Düsseldorf 1972.

Hagopian, J. V./Dolch, M., eds.: Insight I, Analyses of American Literature, Frankfurt 1967.

Lubbers, Klaus: Typologie der Short Story, Darmstadt 1977.

Rohmer, Ludwig: Theorie der Kurzgeschichte, Wiesbaden 1976[2].

3. Reading Short Stories in English Classes

Bludau, M.: Die Rolle der Lektüre auf der Sekundarstufe I – Englisch. In: Neusprachl. Mitteilungen 30 (1977), S. 129–136.

Brusch, W./Köhring, K. H.: Von der Textschlüsselung zur Textverarbeitung. In: Der fremdsprachl. Unterricht, Heft 39, 1976, S. 2–13.

Freese, P./Groene, H./Hermes, L. (eds.): Die Short Story im Englischunterricht der Sekundarstufe II, Paderborn 1979.

Freese, Peter: Zur Erstellung von Textsequenzen für den Englischunterricht der reformierten Sekundarstufe II. In: Praxis d. Neusprachl. Unterrichts 1, 1980, S. 22–34.

Hermes, Liesel: Von der gelenkten zur selbständigen Texterschließung: Lektüren im Englischunterricht der Sekundarstufe I. In: Der fremdsprachl. Unterricht, Heft 51, 3/1979, S. 2–15.

Glaap, A. R.: Linguistische Aspekte des Lektüreeinsatzes in der Sekundarstufe I des Gymnasiums. In: Der fremdsprachl. Unterricht, Heft 51, 3/1979.

Mihm, E.: Akademische und schulische Interpretation, Praxis d. Neusprachl. Unterrichts 1, 1966, S. 90 ff.

Stockebrand, M./Nadorf, B.: Unterrichtsschritte auf dem Weg zur selbständig angefertigen Interpretation von erzählenden Texten. In: Der fremdsprachl. Unterr., Heft 64, 1982, S. 295–305 (mit Interpretationsschema).

4. Cassettes

The Early Short Stories of Hemingway
Lecturer: Delbert Wylder
Everett/Edwards, 1976, 35 mins.

The Middle Short Stories of Hemingway
Lecturer: Delbert Wylder
Everett/Edwards, 1976, 42 mins.

The Late Short Stories of Hemingway
Lecturer: Delbert Wylder
Everett/Edwards, 1976, 40 mins.

A Look at Ernest Hemingway
Released by the Center for Cassette Studies, 1975. 5 cassettes: 34 mins, 25 mins, 26 mins, 25 mins, 26 mins.

(available through the Amerikahäuser)